My Memoirs Completed
"Al Takmilah"

King Abdallah of Jordan

Translated from the Arabic by Harold W. Glidden

With a foreword by
His Majesty King Hussein Ibn Talal of Jordan

Longman
London and New York

This Work is a complete translation of *Al-Takmilah*
by King 'Abdallah ibn al-Husayn
published by an anonymous publication committee
in Amman, Jordan, 1951

LONGMAN GROUP LTD
London

Associated companies, branches and representatives
throughout the world.

© Longman Group Ltd 1978

First published 1978

ISBN 0 582 78082 9

British Library Cataloguing in Publication Data

Abdallah, *King of Jordan*
    My memoirs completed (al-Takmilah).
    1. Abdallah, *King of Jordan* 2. Jordan –
    Kings and rulers – Biography
    I. Title
    956.95′04′0924   DS154.53   77–30750

ISBN 0–582–78082–9

Printed in Great Britain by
Whitstable Litho Ltd., Whitstable, Kent

Contents

A Foreword
By His Majesty King Hussein Ibn Talal of Jordan

My grandfather, the late King Abdallah Ibn Al-Husayn, founder of the Hashemite Kingdom of Jordan, was by any criterion of evaluation a unique and towering figure in the newly emerging, turbulent, fascinating, and often tragic unfolding of events which characterized the awakening of the contemporary Arab World.

The process is as yet unfinished, and is inherently unamenable to completion, because the life of nations, particularly in the present dynamic world, is an on-going flow which has no identifiable beginning and, likewise, no foreseeable end.

But there are landmarks along this arduous, meandering journeying which can be recognized. My late grandfather was certainly one of those landmarks. His career was abundant and multi-dimensional. It would be difficult, even for those who had the most intimate and prolonged association with him, to single out any specific area of activity or endowment with which his memory, as reflected in his career and partly registered in his memoirs and in the *Supplement* which is the subject of this foreword, could be stamped.

He was a humanist, a man of letters, a statesman of the highest calibre, a warrior, a leader of men, a nation-builder, a visionary and a deeply religious man.

As a son of the Hijaz and of the Arabian Peninsula, he was to a degree a traditionalist, deeply imbued with the morals, mores and values of Arab society, in their unadulterated form. But he was equally a product of the modern world, having obtained his higher education and, later, having lived and served in Istanbul as elected deputy of Mecca in the Ottoman Mabuthan (parliament). The Ottoman Empire was then one amongst a handful of world empires, albeit a waning empire, whose ultimate demise came about in the wake of its defeat in World War I, when it had allied itself with the European Central Powers, against the more sagacious and sincere advice of Sherif Husayn ibn Ali, the overlord of Mecca and the Hijaz.

King Abdallah's character and experience constituted a unique admixture and a confluence of the two streams, the traditionalist and the modern. In his private life, he was devoutly attached to his early traditionalist upbringing, with its stable norms, its poetry, its simplicity and its genuineness. His nostalgia for that form of life was never diluted or undermined by his extensive encounters with the intricacies and the fundamental forces of modern civilization. My hunch is that he would have preferred the former, at least emotionally. But my grandfather was too shrewd, too far-sighted and pragmatic a man not to perceive that the old ways, in a forbidding, ever-changing, and shrinking world, were a thing of the past, which could no longer be sustained and were doomed to an irretrievable fading away. Hence, his public career, whether in statecraft, war or diplomacy, was predominantly forward-looking, open and modern. In a world where only the fittest survive, a continual surging forward was the only avenue to survival, and his dynamic personality was such that he would not settle for less. He was among the first Arab leaders to adopt a system of constitutional democracy derived from his personal experience of the need for the participation and representation of his people. This was the form of inspiration to which his people looked for direction, and in that he was outward-looking, inexorably frank and extrovert. The awesome challenges which faced him, in a period marked by turbulence, war, intrigues, reverses, and diplomatic complexities – to use an under-statement – did not in the least cow his undauntable spirit. It could be said without reservations that considering the world forces at play and, in many instances, arrayed against him and his sacred cause, and remembering the seemingly incorrigible forces of disarray and the weaknesses which marred Arab society in those incipient years of its awakening from half a millennium of lethargy, his achievements could by no means be underrated. These factors regrettably have so many parallels in contemporary developments in our part of the world attesting further to the perspicacity and wisdom of this great man.

Let us remember that my grandfather was the second son of King Husayn Ibn Ali, whom the Arab nation, half a century ago, had chosen as the standard-bearer and champion of the famed Arab Revolt against Ottoman hegemony, discrimination, and misrule. It was the first truly Arab thrust towards achieving their liberation, unity and progress in modern times. The Arab nation, under the dedicated leadership of Al-Husayn and his sons, fought valiantly, and at great cost and sacrifice, on the side of the Allies, and against their co-religionists the Turks, in the cause of its triumph. The harvest of their long ordeal was bitter, disillusioning, and, in certain instances, tragic.

This was the legacy, or should I more aptly call it the uneasy mission, that King Abdallah Ibn Al-Husayn had inherited, and his genius was that out of the throes of catastrophe he succeeded in salvaging what remnants of the Arab homeland he could, without for one moment losing his revolutionary fervour or his indomitable dedication to the cause of Arab unity.

Throughout the Supplement, al-Takmilah, and in its antecedent the comprehensive and thorough memoirs written over a quarter of a century ago, the dominant theme was his abiding concern for the fulfilment of the original goals and aspirations of the Arab Revolt, which had deviated from its avowed course by internal, but more potently by external forces. The first were inspired by what seemed to him petty, vindictive, and irrelevant counterforces; the second by self-seeking, arrogant, and, in historical perspective, myopic external decisions, which had condemned the Arab homeland east of Suez to artificial and unnatural fragmentation, and consequently to strife and instability.

King Abdallah Ibn Al-Husayn was particularly grieved by the partitioning of natural Syria, in consequence of the Sykes–Picot Agreement, which vivisected natural Syria into zones of mandates and influence between France and Britain. King Abdallah's adversaries, in their relentless and unabashedly self-seeking efforts to abort his efforts towards restoring the God-created and timeless unity and territorial integrity of Syria, tried to denigrate his endeavours by distortive descriptions such as the "Greater Syria Plan", to connote the idea of aggrandisement.

The meeting held at Raghadan Palace on 28 November 1950 between King Abdallah Ibn Al-Husayn and the then Prime Minister of Syria, Dr Nazim Al-Kudsi, is an eloquent and definitive testimony to how two leaders, embracing the same ideals of Syrian unification within an overall Arab unity, approached their common aim.

King Abdallah was unflinching, single-minded, dedicated, and willing to bear every sacrifice towards achieving that cherished goal. He almost took its imperative inevitability for granted, as do truly committed believers in a cause in which they ardently believe. He lectured and taunted his honoured guest on the elemental historical and compelling factors of the situation. King Abdallah was thoroughly well-versed in history, both past and contemporary, and this was in my opinion his mainstay and the fountain-source of the strength which sustained him in the unwavering pursuit of his mission.

Dr Kudsi, highly educated, articulate, and presumably dedicated to the cause, was ambivalent and evasive, and indulged in side issues pertaining to the chronic inter-Arab rivalries and quarrels.

Herein lies the difference between nation-builders, history makers and men of decision such as King Abdallah was, and the conventional politicians, sophisticated as they may be, who, at crucial moments in history, put expediency above the more lasting national causes and destiny of their people.

I would not wish to be too harsh in my assessment of Dr Kudsi's performance. In all probability, he himself was not a free agent within the power-structure prevailing in his country during those years. In making the invidious comparison which I have just made, I am focusing my analysis on the much wider circle of conventional, mediocre, and oftentimes self-seeking politicians who lacked the will, the imagination, or even the true fidelity to the cause which had given them the reins of power in their respective countries and entrusted them with their destiny.

I may add that the comparison, to the generality of readers, is solely of historical significance, important primarily to the special-ized historian of that era.

To me, it is much more significant than that, because it is still a very pervasive phenomenon, which has brought disaster upon the destiny and the welfare of our nation, and has brought about a situation where the very inviolability of our Arab homeland, deprived of its basic cohesion at the heartland, is in grave jeopardy.

Since my accession to the Throne of the Kingdom a quarter of a century ago, I have struggled with all the means at my disposal to continue on the path of Arab unity, in a genuine effort to fulfil the aims and aspirations for which my grandfathers had dedicated their lives. It is with profound regret that I find myself compelled to state that the same forces of negativism, disarray and selfishness, which had obstructed the efforts of earlier generations, are still very much evident and active. Persons and personalities have in many instances changed; but erroneous orientations and malicious machinations have not. Nevertheless it has been Jordan's destiny, central as it is to the developments in our area, to strive realistically for Arab cohesion. It is only through these factors that the turbulent Arab World can move towards the stability, prosperity and peace that its people so greatly deserve.

The *Takmilah* is not a chronological orderly register of events, in the traditional forms of diaries or autobiographies. The earlier thorough memoirs qualify under this category. Nor is the *Takmilah* merely topical and selective. It is a combination of both, permeated all through by an analytical and penetrative perception of the underlying causes behind those events.

It could best be characterized as a critique of the Arab character and of the environmental factors which formulated its attitudes, behaviour and actions in those years. This is reflected at the outset, in King Abdallah's introduction to the Supplement under the heading "A Word on the Arabs in General".

Unfortunately, it is not always clear, especially to the uninitiated, whether he was talking about the urban, the beduin, or the rural Arabs. My presumption is that the illustrious King assumed that all Arabs carried the same basic traits, with differences only in degree, depending upon their varying stages of development, and, by corollary, upon the differing environmental influences to which each was subjected.

The absence of clear-cut distinction could not have been an oversight, nor for that matter a lack of discernment. This is because King Abdallah knew the various categories of Arabs intimately and at close range. He had dealt with urban and highly educated Arab personages, just as he had the closest comradeship with naturally endowed and formidable tribal sheikhs. He could deal with both, with deep understanding and incisive judgement.

King Abdallah's undoubted magnanimity is best reflected in his criticisms of friend and adversary alike. Even in his most outspoken moments – and he was sharply outspoken when he felt he should be – he was free of rancour or of hate. This does not of course mean that he was angelic, for he was human after all. But whatever bitterness he displayed was directed against what he regarded as the misdeeds of men rather than against the men themselves. He was intolerant of the shortsighted, the selfish and the outright wicked. But his impulsive as well as his deep-felt reaction was a fervent hope and prayer that their frailties might eventually be rectified. This was perhaps too optimistic, but nonetheless it portrayed his innermost character.

As I stated earlier, some of the events in the Supplement are of transient and passing value, as most memoirs are. It is a register of an era which has long passed. But other issues with which the *Takmilah* dealt are still very much alive and burning, in spite of the passage of over a quarter of a century since King Abdallah wrote it.

I shall single out three major issues in these reflections, which have remained unresolved and challenging, and which constitute the burden and the responsibility of the present and possibly of future generations.

First is the cause of Arab unification on a sound, realistic, and lasting basis. For how many arbitrary unities have collapsed, even before they had seen the dawn of life?

My grandfather's generation took Arab unity for granted, and it was inconceivable to them to find themselves in a state of parochial fragmentation. This is attributable to two facts: first, with rare exceptions they had lived for centuries as citizens of an extensive and unified empire, the Ottoman; when disaffection set in, it was the Arab provinces in unity versus the Turkish. Second, when the Arabs began the process of awakening and the rediscovery of their history, it did not cost them much effort to recognize that their greatness was conterminous with their unity. Their golden ages had been identified with such unified and extensive conglomerations as the Ummayad, the Abbassid, the Fatimid, and other Arab and Islamic Empires. They possessed the ability to hold their own against alien and hostile intrusions. They also possessed the means to contribute abundantly and creatively to world culture and civilization. They were, in fact, in the forefront for many centuries.

King Abdallah Ibn Al-Husayn and his generation of reawakened Arabs were fully cognizant of these historical truths. The basic objective of the Great Arab Revolt was not a negative and vindictive dismantling of the Ottoman Empire, in which, but for its latter-day aberrations, they had been honoured and equal citizens; the basic objective of the Revolt was the re-creation of a unified Arab domain, at least in the Arab East, in which the Arab nation could once more restore its eminence and its creativity, and ensure its inviolability and security. It was for this reason that King Abdallah reacted with impatient vehemence to all those who misconstrued the basic objectives of the Arab Revolt and had the audacity to rationalize their adherence to misguided and disastrous provincialism.

My generation, in contrast with that of my grandfather, faces a steep uphill fight to achieve meaningful unity. The Sykes–Picot fragmentation had not only outlived its authors and the colonial purposes for which they had decreed it; it had also sunk deep roots of provincialism in the consciousness of the people, who are invariably prone to accept the familiar and the prevalent.

Furthermore, vested interests have in the meantime struck roots, and these have an inherent tendency to self-perpetuation.

It was against these forces of distorted traditions that my grandfather had to contend, but to no avail. My task and that of those who share my mission is doubly the more difficult and challenging, and surmounting those forces, to which I am devoting a major part of my life and energies, would be a vindication and a fulfilment of my grandfather's and my people's most cherished aspiration.

Secondly, in my reflections on the Supplement, I shall give some thoughts on a phenomenon which, though universal, is more specifically an Arab trait, or frailty if you wish.

There are always those who can think only in absolutes, and others who believe that the world is based on relational relativity. The criterion in their every judgement is whether what they are seeking is feasible and attainable or not. How many nations have gone down to their ruin because they had failed to equate their ends with their means, their words with their deeds?

My grandfather, as his Supplement clearly testifies, belonged to the pragmatic school, without in any way diluting his intense idealism or his basic dedication to the causes in which he believed.

This, in my opinion, is what spells the difference between success and failure. In war, he was always mindful of the logistics of the situation. In diplomacy and statecraft, he never operated in a cloistered vacuum. He carefully assessed the forces aligned with him and those arrayed against him.

This calculating attitude sometimes made him misunderstood among sections of the uninformed, who are inclined to hear what pleases them, rather than what serves their cause. Such inclination is intensified when wilfully fed into them by self-seeking leaders and fomented by wily adversaries.

King Abdallah spoke out the truth, loudly and vehemently, as he saw it, regardless of whether it pleased or displeased his listeners. The fact that he was ahead of his time in his assessment of situations, and of projecting the possible consequences of every action or inaction, was not solely, or even primarily, intuitive or prophetic. It was largely the accumulated wisdom with which more than half a century of a uniquely rich career had endowed him. Triumphs and reverses, trials and errors, successes and failures, these were his armoury when King Abdallah strove with only partial success to put his vast experience in the service of the Arab cause, at the moment of its greatest need.

I sometimes wonder, with deep sorrow, how different might

have been the destiny of the Middle East if his advice had been heeded in timely and selfless good faith. Is it any wonder then that the Arabs, over the past quarter of a century, and in spite of their considerable potential, have not achieved anywhere near what they should have achieved? With a disunited Arab World, in the real and meaningful sense, with instability more often the rule than the exception, and with regimes changing with the rapidity and regularity of changing seasons, how could any nation go very far?

The reason for giving my thoughts on the two aforementioned subjects is that they constitute a basic theme in the Supplement, and their importance is by no means diminished in our own day. Unity amongst the Arabs and experienced wisdom at the helm are as imperative today as they ever were. King Abdallah would have reacted with profound grief, if he had been alive today, to see that most of his forebodings, warnings and projections had come to pass. It was not in his character to have gleefully said: "I told you so!" His reaction would have been a profound sorrow and infuriation that it should have needed catastrophe to befall his people, when wisdom, experience, and discerning might have averted it all, or at least mitigated its awesome consequences.

A quarter of a century is a relatively long span, even in the life of nations. It would be an error to convey the impression that during this span the Arab World stood stagnant. Far from it, for most of the Arab countries have achieved significant and, in some instances, spectacular advances. King Abdallah would be happily surprised and gratified to see that Jordan has made, and continues inexorably to make, great leaps forward, in all fields and walks of life, through hard work, discipline and dedication.

Its hitherto undreamed of riches and the expanded exploitation of its strategic natural resources, particularly in the field of energy, are bound to transform the whole Arab World beyond recognition and accord it a new and potent status amongst the family of nations.

But, and as I stated earlier in these reflections, everything in the world can only be judged in relative terms. Achievements should be commensurate with the achievements of other nations in similar situations, and also with the challenges which confront us as a nation from quarters close and afar. The yardstick by which we can judge our success or failure must be the measure of the type of premises which King Abdallah's Supplement, in the relatively less complicated circumstances of his era, underscored: namely, Arab cohesion, stability, temperance, continuity, and wisdom. It is my earnest hope and belief that the Arabs are in the process of maturing to conform to those indispensible prerequisites.

Third, in my reflections on The Supplement, is King Abdallah's deep involvement in and concern for the fate of the Palestinian people, as he saw that fate unfold tragically and inexorably over three decades. It is incumbent on me to recall here, if only for the historical record, that his father, the leader of the Great Arab Revolt, King Al-Husayn Ibn Ali, had practically abdicated his throne in the Middle East and the unified Arab domain over which he was to have reconstructed the newly-resurgent Arab nation, because he could not bring himself to accept an alienation of Palestine from the rest of the Arab homeland. His stand was an act of conscience and of morality, let alone what he deeply felt to be an act of incredible and discredited betrayal by his allies, on whose side he had staked the destiny of the whole Arab nation.

His son, King Abdallah, was more cognizant of this fact than anyone else, having been his most intimate and trusted advisor and emissary. It would take more than brief reflections on the Supplement, restricted in scope and purpose, to give adequate coverage and appraisal of King Abdallah's approach to the sordid and, as it turned out, catastrophic fate of Palestine and its people. But a few highlights, which are to be read in the *Takmilah*, would not fail to prove that its fate might have taken a sharply different course if he had been at the helm or at least if his advice, at every stage, had been heeded by those who were.

As is well-known to those familiar with the Middle East, Palestine and Transjordan were one entity, which, in turn, constituted Southern Syria. Mr Winston Churchill, in his capacity as Colonial Secretary in the British cabinet, decided in 1922 that Palestine and Transjordan be severed. As a result of King Abdallah's vigorous and successful efforts, Transjordan was spared the imposition of the British undertaking to establish a Jewish National home in Palestine.

The British Empire, in the aftermath of World War I, was the foremost power in the world. Its decisions were, therefore, irrevocable and unchallenged.

The British decision of separation had advantages as well as disadvantages. The advantages were that it spared Transjordan and its people the imposition of Zionist colonization. The disadvantages were that it entailed a further vivisection of the body-politic of geographic Syria, and consequently a further weakening of the capability of the Palestinian region to more effectively resist the Zionist onslaught. Resistance can take many forms, and not the least of them is wise political decision at crucial turning-points.

It is often said that the Palestine question is a chronicle of missed opportunities. This is partly true, though not entirely. For judging in retrospect, it is my considered opinion, as it was my grandfather's, that the Zionist thrust and avalanche could have been blunted but not entirely thwarted. Morality and power-politics do not, in most instances, match. The tragic undoing and dismantling of the Palestinian people, to which their leadership unwittingly contributed, was that they adamantly refused to understand or accept this unpleasant but elementary fact of life.

King Abdallah was in the unenviable and tantalizing position of watching helplessly the events across the river Jordan, but of being unable to do very much to change their course. He could project and predict the disaster that was in store; he could offer his advice and warnings to the Palestinian as well as to the Arab leaderships of his day; he could plead with and warn the British Government of the dastardly consequences of their mistaken policies. These are on record in his memoirs and in the subsequent Supplement.

But what had rendered his efforts fruitless was that he was deprived of the power of decision-making. Let me cite a few examples to illustrate what I mean. In the aftermath of the 1936 Rebellion by the Arabs of Palestine, fearing, and rightly so, as King Abdallah explained in his messages to the British Government, that the uncontrolled and massive influx of Jewish immigration into Palestine would inevitably result in the destruction and dispersal of the Palestinian people, the British Government sent the Peel Commission to investigate the situation on the spot. In 1937 the Commission recommended the partitioning of Palestine, with the major areas of green Palestine remaining in the hands of its legitimate Palestinian owners. The Palestinian Arab areas were to have united with Transjordan under the stewardship and reign of King Abdallah. The proposed state, which would have been designated The United Arab Kingdom, would have included such famed and ancient cities and towns as Jerusalem – the Old and most of the New – since it was largely Arab; Jaffa, Lydda, Safad, Ramleh, Nazareth, Acre, Beersheba, Asqalan, Gaza, right up to the Egyptian frontier, not to mention the whole of the West Bank.

The Jewish state would have been confined to a narrow coastal strip, extending from Tel-Aviv to Haifa. The so-called moderate leadership amongst the Palestinian Arabs accepted the plan and even initiated talks with King Abdallah for its implementation. The extremist elements within the Palestinian leadership rejected it outright, and since they possessed the gun, their counsel prevailed.

The Zionist leadership, unhappy that their grand design of expansion would be blunted, left it to the Arabs to bear the onus of rejection. The Arabs almost invariably played into their hands. Indeed, the Israelis' anticipation of Arab reactions constituted a basic pillar in their calculations and decision-making. If the Arab leadership was always willing to play the Zionist game, out of ignorance, zealotry, over-confidence, complacency or even misguided selfishness, why should the Zionist leadership be the party to say No?

Another example was King Abdallah's advice to the Palestinian leadership to accept the White Paper, after a round table conference in London in 1939. This would have granted Palestine its full independence, with the Arabs two-thirds in the majority. Again, the extremist Arab leadership rejected the Plan, on the grounds that the Plan included a proviso for a five-year interim period before it went into effect.

The Zionists, likewise, fought it tooth and nail; but in the eyes of the Western world it was the Palestinian Arabs who had thwarted the Plan.

The third example of shortsighted Arab leadership was the inability to take a longer view of the consequences of the United Nations Partition Plan on 29 November 1947. This again could have at least preserved most of the green Palestine – I am excluding the mostly arid desert of the Negev, which comprises half of Palestine – to its Palestinian and legitimate inhabitants.

Arab division and indecision and their disastrous consequences bring me back to my earlier comments on King Abdallah's wise and farsighted pragmatism. He had advised the Palestinian and other Arab leaderships to accept the plan and to continue the struggle, but his advice went unheeded. And when the crunch came, and the Zionists, on the pretext of Arab rejection, launched their carefully-planned design to conquer the whole of Palestine, it was King Abdallah's Jordanian Army which was in the forefront, and which succeeded in salvaging by far the greater part of what could be salvaged in the circumstances.

The more vociferous voices of rejection were sadly absent, to match by deeds their loud words. And to add to the irony of the situation, King Abdallah was assassinated, in one of the holiest shrines of Islam, Al-Aqsa Mosque, and in the Holy City, which his Army alone had saved. And on what pretext by those who were behind the assassin's bullets? That he had betrayed the Palestine cause! When things reach such an abyss of ugly wickedness, I sometimes wonder whether blind irrationality is not a more predominant trait in politics than rationality. Let me set the record straight, clearly and categorically. No country in the world likes to be partitioned, and Palestine is no exception. King Abdallah, a true adherent of his father's mission was, in his innermost soul, as opposed to the alienation of any part of Palestine as anyone else. But to him, moral judgement and personal beliefs were an exercise in futility, unless backed by viable and adequate power, in the broad meaning of the term.

He had perceived the Zionist iceberg and its dimensions, while others had seen only its tip. He makes reference to it in the *Takmilah*. His tactics and strategy were therefore attuned to circumventing and minimizing the possible consequences of a head-on collision. Others saw only the tip, and their responses were over-confidence, inflexibility, and outright complacency. The misfortune of Middle East politics is that all the political forces in the area subsequently stumbled on militarism, leaving the real issues unresolved to the present day.

The strategic depth of the half a million Jews of Palestine – though a minority in the country – was the world Zionist movement, with its pervasive and awesome influence in the world centres of power and decision-making of his era.

Thus, the partition Plan of 1947 was endorsed by practically all the major powers, including the United States and the Soviet Union. How could a million and a quarter disarmed and helpless Palestinians withstand such a formidable combination? That they felt morally right is understandable, but the failure of their leadership to assess the consequences is inexcusable.

The tragedy of the Palestinians was that most of their leaders had paralysed them with false and unsubstantiated promises that they were not alone; that eighty million Arabs and four hundred million Muslims would instantly and miraculously come to their rescue. When the moment of destiny struck, the only assistance forthcoming was a few thousand soldiers from a few contiguous and neighbouring Arab countries, who were outmatched substantially by their adversaries. With hindsight, we can appreciate that many Arab leaders have since asked for, and accepted, far less than what King Abdallah had then proposed.

To me, as to King Abdallah, there is a golden rule in evaluating policy and in taking decisions. The first is "know thyself", for this is pivotal in assessing your capabilities and your limitations. The second is "know the enemy", for failure to do that can spell disaster, and this is precisely what happened to the Palestinian people and their rightful cause.

I would not wish to go much further in my reflections on the *Takmilah*, for it is the work itself which I urge all those interested and concerned to read carefully, to derive the lessons from its message.

It is regrettable that the *Takmilah* does not include some of the inside information, in the crucial period of 1948 to 1951, to which King Abdallah was privy. There are two reasons for this incompleteness. One is that King Abdallah was a very considerate and responsible statesman. He did not wish to embarrass some of his reigning colleagues for their failures and misjudgement, when the dust had not yet settled in the wake of the disastrous consequences which had befallen Palestine and its people. The second is his untimely and tragic passing away, when he was still, in spite of his age, in his full vigour and vitality, both physically and in mental alertness. It is a loss which, I hope, can be retrieved from his records and papers in due course.

My final comment is on the style of the *Takmilah* and on the language of diplomatic discourse which was then in vogue. Today, we have become accustomed to the ways of open diplomacy, with its accompanying vituperative vulgarity and bad taste. The Supplement is perhaps a closing chapter of an era when opinions and articulate ideas did not have to be expressed in other than polite style and language. It was the classical and deferential style which we so largely miss today.

I strongly commend the *Takmilah* of King Abdallah Ibn Al-Husayn to the reader, because it is absorbingly interesting, instructive, and timely, in the prevailing uncertainties and turbulence which continue to envelop the fate and destiny of our part of the world.

Amman

Al-Hussein Ibn Talal

1937: Partition Plan accepted by King Abdallah

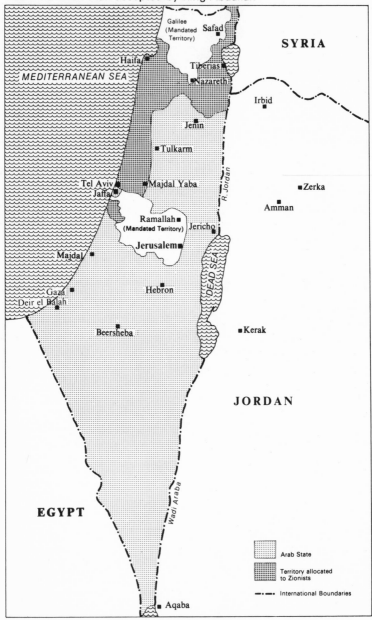

Galilee
(Mandated
Territory) Safad

SYRIA

Haifa

MEDITERRANEAN SEA

Tiberias
■Nazareth

Irbid

Jenin■

■Tulkarm

Tel Aviv
Jaffa

■Majdal Yaba

R. Jordan

■Zerka

Amman■

Ramallah■
(Mandated Territory)

Jericho■

Jerusalem■

Majdal

■

DEAD SEA

Gaza■
Deir el Balah■

Hebron■

Beersheba■

■Kerak

JORDAN

EGYPT

Wadi Araba

Arab State

Territory allocated
to Zionists

─ ∙ ─ ∙ ─ International Boundaries

■ Aqaba

1947: United Nations' Partition Plan

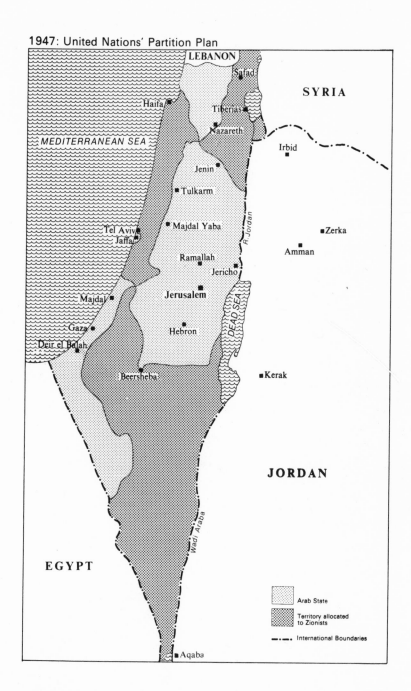

LEBANON

Safad

SYRIA

Haifa

Tiberias

Nazareth

MEDITERRANEAN SEA

Irbid

Jenin

Tulkarm

Zerka

Majdal Yaba

Tel Aviv
Jaffa

Amman

Ramallah

Jericho

Majdal

Jerusalem

DEAD SEA

Gaza

Hebron

Deir el Balah

Kerak

Beersheba

JORDAN

EGYPT

Wadi Araba

R. Jordan

Aqaba

Arab State

Territory allocated
to Zionists

▬ ▪ ▬ ▪ ▬ International Boundaries

1948: Boundaries at the Truce

LEBANON

Safad

SYRIA

Haifa

Tiberias
Nazareth

MEDITERRANEAN SEA

Irbid

Jenin

Tulkarm
Nablus

R. Jordan

Majdal Yaba

Zerka

Tel Aviv
Jaffa

Ramallah

Amman

Jericho

Majdal

Jerusalem

DEAD SEA

Hebron

Gaza
Deir el Balah

Beersheba

Kerak

JORDAN

Wadi Araba

EGYPT

Territories allocated
to Zionists in 1947

Territory seized by
Zionists in 1948

—·—·— International Boundaries

Aqaba

1956: The Suez War

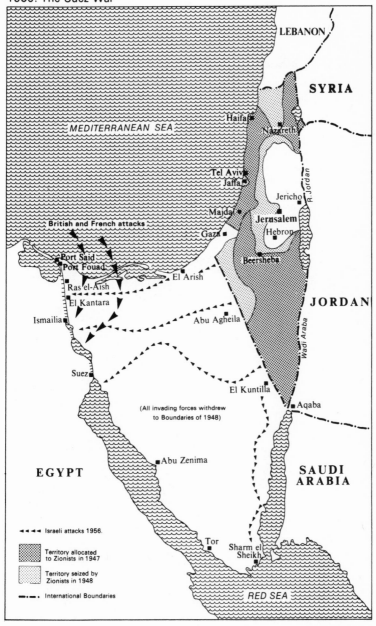

LEBANON

SYRIA

MEDITERRANEAN SEA

Haifa

Nazareth

Tel Aviv

Jaffa

Jericho

R. Jordan

Majdal

Jerusalem

Gaza

Hebron

British and French attacks

Beersheba

Port Said
Port Fouad

Ras el-Aish

El Arish

JORDAN

El Kantara

Ismailia

Abu Agheila

Wadi Araba

Suez

El Kuntilla

Aqaba

(All invading forces withdrew
to Boundaries of 1948)

EGYPT

Abu Zenima

SAUDI
ARABIA

◄ ◄ ◄ Israeli attacks 1956.

Territory allocated
to Zionists in 1947

Tor

Sharm el
Sheikh

Territory seized by
Zionists in 1948

— ■ — ■ International Boundaries

RED SEA

1967: The June War

LEBANON

SYRIA

Haifa Nazareth

Irbid

MEDITERRANEAN SEA

Tel Aviv
Jaffa

Jericho

R. Jordan

Amman

Majdal
Gaza

Jerusalem
Hebron

DEAD SEA

Beersheba

Port Said
Port Fouad

El Arish

Ras el-Aish

JORDAN

Suez Canal

El Kantara

Ismailia

Abu Agheila

Wadi Araba

SINAI

Suez

El Kuntilla

Aqaba

Abu Zenima

EGYPT

SAUDI
ARABIA

Territories allocated
to Zionists in 1947

Territory seized by
Zionists in 1948

Territory seized by
Israel in 1967

International Boundaries

Tor
Sharm el
Sheikh

RED SEA

xxii

1973: The October War

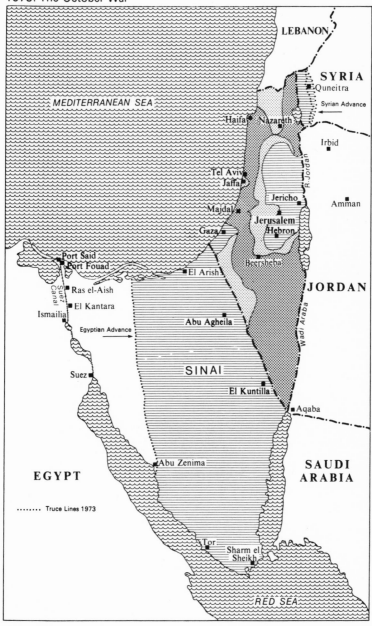

- MEDITERRANEAN SEA
- LEBANON
- SYRIA
- Quneitra
- Syrian Advance
- Haifa
- Nazareth
- Irbid
- Tel Aviv
- Jaffa
- R. Jordan
- Jericho
- Amman
- Majdal
- Jerusalem
- Hebron
- Gaza
- Beersheba
- Port Said
- Port Fouad
- El Arish
- JORDAN
- Suez Canal
- Ras el-Aish
- El Kantara
- Ismailia
- Egyptian Advance
- Abu Agheila
- Wadi Araba
- Suez
- SINAI
- El Kuntilla
- Aqaba
- EGYPT
- Abu Zenima
- SAUDI ARABIA
- ········ Truce Lines 1973
- Tor
- Sharm el Sheikh
- RED SEA

Introductory Note

In the interest of consistency and exactitude, it has been thought advisable to observe uniformly the scientific system of transliteration, used generally by Arabists in the United States, for all Arabic personal names, and also for place names except in those cases where there exists a commonly accepted English spelling. The Arabic original is unannotated, but it has been considered necessary in this edition to clarify many otherwise obscure or unclear references in the text. The annotation throughout is the work of the translator.

Note by the Publication Committee

Five years ago there were revealed to the world memoirs[1] containing the most important material which mankind has read about the life of this great man, replete as they were with historical events and calamities and following as they did in an unbroken line the history of the whole Arab people in their various countries and states. These were the memoirs of His Hashimite Majesty King 'Abdallah ibn al-Husayn, heir of the renaissance of the Arabs and pillar of their house.

These memoirs were received with acclaim and admiration both in the East and in the West. Therefore, as the years passed and other great events took place in the Arab World, people turned to the author of those memoirs and requested him to enlarge upon what he had already discussed, written, and witnessed. He was kind enough to accede to this desire (may God uphold his reign and grant glory to his army!) and has written these eternal new pages entitled *Completion of My Memoirs*.

The Publication Committee again is honoured in presenting this completion to the world. It thanks His Majesty for his kindness and help and prays High and Almighty God to preserve His Majesty as a solid pillar and firm support for the Arabs and Islam and as a beacon for guidance, knowledge, and light.

Amman, 1 January 1951

---

[1] Two Arabic versions of *Mudhakkarati,* as the original is called, were published: one in 1945 and one in 1947. An incomplete and reworked English translation by G. Khuri of Haifa, edited by Philip P. Graves, was published in London in 1950 under the title *Memoirs of King Abdullah of Transjordan.* For reviews of this see *The Middle East Journal,* vol. 5, no. 2 (Spring, 1951), pp. 251–252, and *The Muslim World,* vol. 42 (January 1952), pp. 76–77.

Preface

No sensible person should write of anything which he does not know or understand or speak of that which does not concern him. The memoirs I have dictated to my private secretary reflect the events of past days in which I strove to the best of my ability with pen, tongue, and sword for the good of the Arabs. In so doing I had a number of goals: the development of a national consciousness and its elevation to the height of Arab independence; the preservation of that character without which the Arabs can never rise to mastery and prosperity; and finally, to liberate the Arabs from those self-seeking and power-hungry compatriots of theirs who neither understand them nor know how to govern them. For the Arabs in their present state are like a man who is totally paralysed. Although he is aware of what is going on he cannot restore his limbs to movement; nevertheless he feels no pain, because the deadening effect of the paralysis numbs his limbs.

The paralysis of the Arabs lies in their present moral character. They are satisfied with little, hence cannot attain great things; they are obsessed with tradition and concerned only with profit and the display of oratorical patriotism. If you question any one of them about Arabism and its history or about the Arab lands and their extent he stops dead like a sheikh's donkey on a steep hill.

Such is the Arabs' evil fortune; the wheel of time rolls unceasingly on and others are already many laps ahead of them. Perhaps the reader will find harshness and bitterness in these words and wonder how I could have written them. It is because I have been driven by a small remaining spark of hope for my miserable people, a hope that is due to their inherent characteristic of self-esteem. So if any Arab should be moved by the demands of this self-esteem and the bestirring of his pride to shake from himself the dust of baseness, greed, cowardice, and avarice and push forward with humility and steadfastness of purpose with his face turned toward the light, it would be the way in which I had hoped to see the Arabs react, God willing.

These are the first words that I have dictated to my private secretary Ghazi ibn Raji, whom I wish to commend for the understanding and careful attention which he has displayed and for his encouraging me to speak frankly and unhesitatingly. I must mention also my faithful and cherished friend 'Abd al-Mun'im al-Rifa'i, my present Minister to Iran and Pakistan, for the hand he has lent in arranging the contents of these memoirs and checking the text. For it is well known among my friends that I find it distasteful to check anything which I have written and am done with; so it is he who is the arbiter of the success of this arduous task.

These memoirs are divided into several chapters, which deal with: the Arab League – how it was created, what the Arabs understand it to be, and how it is viewed by its member states; the Palestine war, a bit of its history, and the question of the unified Arab command – without my going into certain confidential matters the publication of which would benefit no one except troublemakers who wish the Arabs no good; and the activities of the Arab Higher Committee and the member governments of the Arab League regarding the Palestine case. This discussion deals also with the question of the internationalization of the Holy Places and the unity of the eastern and western banks of the Jordan. A special chapter is devoted to Great Britain's Arab policy, which if correctly understood and properly implemented would benefit all parties concerned for a long time to come. Finally, I have considered also Egypt and North Africa as well as Syria and Jordan. I ask God's help and favour in all this and pray that it may be an admonition and a reminder to my people.

Introduction

A Word on the Arabs in General

Certain of my good British friends who have read my previously-published volume of memoirs have remarked that it was rambling, prolix, lacking in cohesion, and without any clearly defined objective or recommendation for a line of action which the Arabs should follow.

My reply is that I wrote these memoirs for the Arabs as my testimonial to them of the efforts I had made on their behalf and of my genuine concern for their welfare. In them I ascribed the blunders and excesses committed by the Arabs to the fact that they took over the reins of authority while they were still inexperienced and lacking in knowledge. This taking-over of authority had been their goal, but it was also the source of their weakness. If I were familiar with the English language I should like to have completed my memoirs in that tongue and expressed my thoughts fully to those who have shown an interest in them, for the enlightenment of both their friends and their enemies. But English is a strange tongue to me, a fact I most deeply regret. Nevertheless, I am an Arab and I feel that I have some talent for expression, whether to anger or to please my reader; in either case, however, I speak nothing but the truth.

But regarding the inquiry of my British friends as to why I did not bring my memoirs up to date, I must reply that the obstacle lay in the fact that Arab thought at the time was insufficiently developed to appreciate them. As an indication of this I may mention that no Arab has urged me to complete them, as have my British friends; on the contrary, certain self-interested Arab parties have tried to keep this book from seeing the light of day. I must therefore speak out, but at the same time I ask the forgiveness of my people for anything I say that might hurt their feelings.

The Arab has a penchant for unfettered liberty and cannot abide restriction or restraint. This is the reason why he is associated with the desert and the steppe and exhibits an incomparable bravery in

1

defending his possessions. He is courageous and fond of oratory as well as poetry and love. Often he may be seen in the heat of the day taking refuge under his *abaya* from the burning sun and the intense heat of the earth. Or at night he may be heard singing to the beauty of the stars of heaven, should there not be at hand any black-eyed, high-born daughter of his race to reciprocate; of such is the origin of most of the Arabs. The tribes of the Shammar confederation, whose grazing grounds extend from the Jazirah of Syria, bordering on Kurdistan and Turkey in the north, southward to the twin mountains of Tayyi'; the tribes of the 'Anazah, the most numerous of all Arab tribes, ranging from Syria to the Hijaz; and finally the 'Amr of the Sharah region of southern Jordan and the Sarah who extend as far as the Yemen; all these, as both others and I myself know, lack even the barest elements of education and must face the future as best they can.

For the benefit of the reader I shall identify the largest tribes, all of which are in the same state they found themselves in during the Middle Ages, and I shall give an estimate of their numbers. I have already mentioned the Shammar, who range from Jabal Sinjar in northern Iraq to an area south of Ha'il, which town was the capital of their amirs of the house of Rashid whose power was recently destroyed[1] and whose territories were forcibly annexed by King Ibn Sa'ud. This tribe is estimated at about 50,000 souls. To the south and east of the Shammar are the 'Ilwah and Burayh clans of the Mutayr; these are the people who have taken up their abode at al-Artawiyah southeast of Ha'il, in accordance with the Wahhabi plan of settling the tribes. Then there are the 'Alawiyin Mutayr, known as the Banu 'Abdallah, who number about 20,000 souls. To the east of these lie the Hutaym, who are found in the area extending from the vicinity of Tayma' to the eastern part of the lava fields (*harrah*) of Medina and whose numbers are estimated at 15,000. South of these, situated between the 'Utaybah, the Shammar, the Banu 'Abdallah referred to above, and the Hutaym, are the Harb of Najd; they are about 20,000 and include the Banu Salim, the Masruh, and the Banu 'Ali. The 'Utaybah, who are found to the south of the Harb group, number about 40,000 persons.

In addition to these major tribes are smaller ones such as the Banu Harith, the Subay', and the Baqum, in addition to the Subay' of al-Jafrah, who live east of the Hijaz and south of al-'Arid. Next come the Shahran of al-'Aridah, a folk living both in the mountains and in the plains and numbering about 10,000 souls. The tribes of

[1] This took place in 1921.

Qahtan are extremely numerous, perhaps equal to the 'Anazah, and extend as far as the edge of al-Rab' al-Khali (the Empty Quarter). The tribes of the Yemen, on the other hand, are town- and village-dwelling, as are those of the Hijaz from the Saudi-Yemen border to Jordan. Those of the Hijaz include perhaps 2,000,000 persons, while those of the Yemen are between 3,500,000 and 4,000,000 in number and have not progressed beyond the state in which they were living in the Middle Ages. One must not forget the Wuld Sulayman and the Wuld 'Ali of the 'Anazah, which are nomadic tribes comprising 8,000 souls. The tribes and peoples of Kuwait, the amirates of the Persian Gulf, and the protectorates bordering on the Indian Ocean formerly had connections with the government of British India, but now, I believe, these are under the Colonial Office. All of this population together numbers perhaps 1,500,000.

Such, in brief, is the basic Arab stock. I am not aware that there exists either in Iraq or Syria any interest in settling the tribes and providing them with land and education with a view to bringing them to participate in the service of their country and their faith. The reason for this, I fear, is that the present rulers want to keep the desert dwellers in ignorance so that they can continue to dominate and control them. This is the malady from which the Arabs suffer.

The town-dwellers represent a group of those who have spoken Arabic since the rise of the Arabs in the distant past. They, however, have lost the true Arab feeling and have become confused and insensible, striving like the others for personal gain and self-aggrandizement. Instead of putting forth an effort to open up a path for themselves and their people toward true knowledge and riches, they have spent the extensive resources which they once had in an attempt to bring back their lost power and glory. I should not be just, however, if I denied what those emigrants to America from Lebanon, Bethlehem, Bayt Jala, and Ramallah have accomplished. For in truth they have raised aloft the light and fame of the Arabs in the New World, the land of individual effort and work where human liberty and free competition are not denied; it is they who are most worthy of praise and who have the greatest hope for the future. It is because of these considerations that I previously refrained from discussing those matters which have been raised by my friends in the courteous and gentle manner characteristic of British criticism.

Although a certain amount of education has become diffused among the Arabs of the present day, the level of learning in Arab

3

urban centres varies widely. The younger generation has turned for its studies to a variety of scattered and dissimilar colleges and universities where they have absorbed differing ideas, conflicting opinions, and a multiplicity of types of education. I consider unity of education and culture to be just as great a necessity as the political unity of the Arab lands and people. It is imperative also that the level of education in the Hijaz, Najd, and the Yemen be raised to that of modern nations; Islam would be no barrier to expansion in this field. Likewise, it is incumbent upon Egypt to free itself from moral corruption and equalize the distribution of land between the landowners and the miserable and poverty-stricken people. It is the duty of all Arabs to bear witness to the world that they possess a place and constitute an entity among the nations of the world and that they stand today at the side of the democracies in the contest between fear-inspiring communism and popular democracy. To this end the Arabs should postpone the settlement of their differences with the democracies until such time as there is a greater degree of peace than at present, when the hearts of men are filled with fear for the future of the whole world.

The Arabs: the Rulers and the Ruled

In the days before Islam the Arabs had no institutions of government. Possible exceptions were to be found in the Yemen; in southern Syria, where the Ghassanid kingdom[2] existed under the aegis of the Emperor of Byzantium; in Iraq, where the house of al-Mundhir[3] ruled as a satellite of Persia; and in Mecca and the tribe of Quraysh, which possessed something resembling a republic in which an assembly dealt with matters relating to internal order, the pilgrimage, and the preservation of the peace during the pilgrimage season. Since the Arabs did not fight or quarrel within the bounds of the sacred territory, the administration of the pilgrimage area was better organized than the administration in any other Arab country; the regime was stable and administrative decisions were fixed.

With the advent of the divine gift and light of Islam the Arab lands were enlightened, and the basis of God's truth was established and made manifest. The principles were laid down that rule belonged to God alone, that the Koran and the way (*sunnah*) of the Prophet constituted the basis of all conduct, and that God's authority alone was sovereign over men. By this means Islam

[2] This dynasty flourished in the 6th century AD.

[3] This dynasty ruled from the 4th to the 6th century AD. Its capital was at al-Hirah.

4

gathered the scattered Arabs and subjected them to the divine law and the regime of Islam. The pillars of their state were set up and they were rendered capable of carrying out the religious and secular tasks which had been prescribed for them: the reform of morals, the rectification of commercial ethics, the improvement of crafts-manship in industry, and the dissemination of this religious light and order throughout the world.

The Arabs are a people formed in the mould of absolute freedom; one might call this the freedom of the Bedouin, which is basically the liberty to do as one likes without any outside restriction. Islam bound the Arabs with its traditions and way of life and prepared them to serve humanity with a spiritual culture based on a law that confirmed, completed, and protected the divinely-given laws which had preceded it. For the true believer believes in both the Old and the New Testament, in the scriptures of Abraham, and in the revelations which the Koran mentions as having been given to various apostles. It is the summarization of all the divinely-given faiths and it has liberated man from the bonds and shackles with which he was fettered before the coming of Islam. The Arabs, therefore, are now existing in a state of lethargy; they must awaken from it and return to the original goal which was set for them. The democracy toward which the Western nations are striving today and which the Muslims are adopting is already to be found in all its perfection and virtue in Islam; but is it the fault of Islam if the Muslims have ignored and abandoned it? Furthermore, all the advantages claimed for communism by the poor and under-privileged advocates of that creed are to be found in Islam: the tithe, the duty of almsgiving, the claim which the beggar and the underprivileged have on the wealth of the rich, and the expiation of murder by the freeing of a slave before the payment of blood-money. What democracy can boast of anything better than this? What communist system imposes such an obligation on the rich without at the same time treating them unfairly vis-à-vis the poor? Unfortunately, the poor in Islam are many, for the tithe is no longer collected, alms have ceased to be given, and the rights of the mendicant and the destitute are denied.

If one can believe what one hears about communism, the poor under its regime are deprived of everything, even their human rights; they have no freedom of movement and are fed like cattle. As I see it, the world is proceeding to the point where the wheels of daily life will be stalled by such things as the dreadful national-ization movement espoused by socialist democracy, which likewise saps individual initiative and effort. If the situation is as I have stated then who, pray tell, can be expected to exert intellectual effort toward an objective that will be crushed between the upper millstone of nationalizing socialism and the nether millstone of world communism? In such a case a man becomes like a worn-out nag pulling a wagon alongside a harness-mate in the best of condition; the stronger of the two pulls not only his own share of the load but also the weight of his companion. I believe that the light has already begun to dawn on the more intelligent among us; the Arabs must lend each other a helping hand, reach an understanding on the basis of the Islamic principles they have abandoned, and work for the establishment of a community with their Muslim brethren in all lands, in order that they may preserve both peace and their Muslim faith and constitute a force for the service of Islam.

Chapter 1
The Arab World Today

The Arab League: Its Origin and Development

The Arab League represents a concept that was first adumbrated by Nuri Pasha al-Sa'id, then seized upon by Mustafa al-Nahhas Pasha and supported by Mr Antony Eden.[1] It is a sack into which seven heads have been thrust – the Yemen, Najd,[2] Iraq, Syria, Lebanon, Egypt, and Transjordan – with remarkable haste and at a time when Syria and Lebanon were still under a French mandate, Transjordan under a British mandate, and Iraq and Egypt bound by still-valid treaties with Great Britain. Thus the Arab states, with the exception of the Yemen and Najd, were hampered by mandatory and treaty restrictions. Because of this there ensued a remarkable competition between those members of the League which were unencumbered and those which were labouring under various impediments, whether foreign occupation, treaties, or simply ignorance. The Arab countries themselves are content both with the veil concealing that which they wish to hide and with vainglorious boasting about what they wish to advertise. The well-disposed foreigner looks upon the League as the best instrument for the perpetuation of mandates and the treaty regime, but I shall leave it to others to judge the validity of this point of view.

Nuri al-Sa'id was a participant in the Arab Revolt from its beginning to its end. After its conclusion he remained in Syria with King Faysal until the fall of Damascus to the French; at the time of the declaration of Syria's independence he was an active member of the Iraqi Parliament and he is now a well-known cabinet minister.

Al-Nahhas Pasha is like a pillar of light, and it is a source of regret to me that we have not seen eye to eye since the unification of Arab Palestine and Jordan. Though al-Nahhas Pasha is a leader in Egypt, he knows little of the other Arab countries, for the contest between the Wafd and the other Egyptian parties has blinded him to

[1] In his Mansion House speech of 29 May 1941.
[2] By "Najd" or "Najd and the Hijaz" King 'Abdallah means Saudi Arabia.

7

everything except Egypt. He obviously believes that any opposition or undercurrent in Egypt is weaker than his own nerves and that what he has attained time and again in his own country can be attained in any of the Arab countries. The truth, however, is that Egypt and the Arab countries are two different things, and while he may be al-Nahhas Pasha in Egypt he is not al-Nahhas Pasha in the Arab countries.

'Azzam Pasha is a warrior in the Ottoman tradition, a fighter for Tripolitania and Libya, Secretary General of the Arab League, and at the same time an Egyptian by nationality. For Egypt's sake he would not hesitate to destroy anything, even his own son, which might stand in his way; such is the duty of every man who values his own and his country's security. As the saying goes, "Begin with thyself and then with thy brother."

Constructive results might nevertheless be obtained if the Arab chiefs of state could only meet and confer on Arab problems and use their talents to overcome their difficulties. Such a course, I believe, would be their salvation. Instead of doing this, the League's agenda is sent out by its bureau chiefs, without any previous notice, study, or consideration, to the various ministers of the Arab states. They must meet and discuss matters to which they have given no previous thought or attention. An example of this is the collective security pact. It is my opinion that such a pact would be of no benefit unless the chiefs of staff of the Arab states were to give their opinion on it after having been informed of the military strength of each Arab state, its capabilities for contributing to such security, its financial strength, and its reserves of ammunition; only then could they tell how much any given Arab state could contribute to such a security pact. These observations should be brought to the attention of all the foreign ministers and defence ministers of the Arab states.

As for myself, in my capacity as chief and king of the state of Jordan I should make a mutual security pact only with Egypt and Iraq. I imagine, for example, that the Yemen's need for security is confined solely to internal matters; this was made clear at the time of the shameful murder of the late Imam Yahya.[3] Jordan supported the present Imam[4] and he succeeded in suppressing the rebellion. The Yemen needs no guarantee against attack from without since it has no strong enemy at present; Ethiopia is a peaceful state and Egypt is a member of the Arab League, as is Saudi Arabia. Britain's differences with the Yemen need only mutual understanding and

[3] In January 1948.
[4] Imam Ahmad.

knowledge for a solution. What has been said of the Yemen applies also to Saudi Arabia, since the action in Palestine confirmed the fact that the Yemen was unable to send any troops whatever to Palestine. Likewise, the tribal forces despatched to Palestine by Saudi Arabia were incorporated into the Egyptian Army and did not issue a single communiqué in their own name during the fighting. Both Saudi Arabia and the Yemen are still in the same condition militarily as they were at that time, so how can they participate in any guarantee of mutual security?

With Iraq and Egypt a guarantee of mutual security could be arranged on the basis of the already-mentioned conditions: a thorough understanding and clarification of financial and military capabilities and of the means and possibilities of implementing such a guarantee, as well as an understanding that no one of the three countries involved would desert the others as Egypt did when it signed the armistice at Rhodes.[5]

All of these problems should be taken into consideration by those who make such a collective security pact. There will be time enough to think of including Syria and Lebanon after the Syrian Army has been purged and stabilized and a Lebanese Army has been created.

The Palestine Problem

The problem of Palestine and the events that have followed in its train constitute a catastrophe which has befallen the Arabs in their latter days. The Jews, for their part, were united, and they co-operated in bringing immigrants into the country, in building it up, and in striving to free themselves from British control and finally to rule themselves. Likewise the Arabs were united in agreement to support that group which had rebelled against the policy in Palestine for thirty years without endeavouring to understand the Jewish aims or the tenacity of purpose that guided Zionism. It was owing to the verbal blustering of Arab policy, defence by word instead of by deed, the asking of favours from those who preferred the Balfour Declaration to the rights of the Arabs in Palestine, and support of the ex-Mufti and his followers, that the situation was climaxed by Palestine's falling into the hands of the enemy.

As the Palestine issue entered its final stages and the British

[5] The reference is to the armistice with Israel signed at Rhodes on 24 February 1949. This was the first of the Arab armistices with Israel.

announced their decision to withdraw, the Jewish aggression against the Arab parts of Palestine grew serious. The Arabs, on their part, completed the formation of the *Jaysh al-Inqadh* (Army of Deliverance), the subsequent history of which is well known.[6] In its wake followed the Arab military demonstration and the improvised decision to send to Palestine forces that the Arab military leaders had previously declared to be inadequate. Unity of command existed in name only and the Commander in Chief[7] was not permitted to inspect the forces which were supposed to be under him. The Arab troops entered Palestine and their lack of progress, their confusion and absence of preparation, were complete; this was followed by the armistice at Rhodes and those clandestine events which are known to everybody. If it were not necessary to keep certain things confidential out of brotherly feeling and hope for the future, I could support my statements with irrefutable documents and testimonials; I could mention what befell Palestine and its people at the hands of its leaders and those member states of the Arab League which put confidence in these leaders and supported them. History will record the consequences with pain and regret; the grandsons of these men will blush with shame at the deeds of their grandsires.

The development of events connected with the Palestine problem has continued apace. As I have been writing this completion of my memoirs there have taken place here and there certain actions and provocations which have tried the patience of the countries signatory to the armistice in Palestine, but these have been received with calm and steadfastness. It is well known that the Israel side is attempting to have recourse to acts of provocation in order to draw the Arab side into offering defensive resistance for which the Zionists could then represent themselves before the United Nations as not responsible. This does not mean, however, that the Arabs are in a position which requires them to hesitate to carry out their responsibilities in whatever manner may be necessary.

For some time rumours have been circulating regarding inclinations here and there toward reconciliation. As I stated prior to 15 May 1948, I do not want injustice, but when I am called to the defence of the homeland I shall come forward. This I did in fulfilment of my promise, for, as I said, "If they incline toward peace then do you incline toward peace also, and put your trust in

[6] This force is usually known as the Arab Liberation Army. It was commanded by Fawzi al-Qawuqji and sponsored by the Arab League.

[7] King 'Abdallah himself.

God."[8] I had been expecting that a solution to the situation would be found either by agreement or by individual action if there should prove to be no hope of leading the Arabs to pursue a policy of realism; this was both logical and wise. The parties concerned would then be either in a state of actual war or in one of peace and reconciliation; the matter could never be straightened out except on this basis. It is apparent to the whole world from the present situation in Europe that nations and peoples want to put an end both to the state of war between Germany and the democracies and to the cold war between the democracies and communism. War and peace are two things that mankind will continue to experience until the Resurrection, just as season follows season – summer, autumn, winter, and spring – and as day follows night; it is the way of God with His creation. It is the wise man who recognizes danger and repels it either by force or by cunning. But he who remains unprepared either for war or for peace awaits the hour when the spirit departs from his body.

God is my witness that I have never spared any effort to draw to the attention of the Arabs and the representatives of their governments those things wherein the general good, the interest of the fatherland, and the welfare of Palestine itself lay. Nevertheless, all this fell on deaf ears, and damage and injury continued to befall Palestine and its people. Here, for example, are samples of messages I sent to Prince Faysal Al Sa'ud and His Excellency Riyad Bey al-Sulh when they were in Paris attending the United Nations session in 1948:

His Highness Prince Faysal Al Sa'ud, Paris:
   I am making it clear to the Arab League delegates in Paris that I have not refused to accept the creation of a Palestinian state, but I have rejected preventing the people of Palestine from choosing for themselves whatever form of government they may desire after the victory has been won. If I should accept an all-Palestine state before the struggle has ended favourably, the people would make a laughing-stock of me. Nevertheless, I fear that the members of the United Nations might agree to set up such a state just as some of them have accepted the claims of the Jews, with the result that partition might be carried out.
   I am with the Arabs whether they continue in their decision to wage war or whether they preserve the *status quo*. The other alternative would be to act upon the decision of the United Nations, not the proposals of

[8] Koran 8:63.

11

Bernadotte. When the United Nations has rendered its verdict the League should convene and decide what must actually be done.

My greetings to you all.

'Abdallah ibn al-Husayn

Amman, 30 September 1947 [*sic*, for 1948]

His Excellency Riyad Bey al-Sulh, Paris:
The report of Count Bernadotte was never submitted to me for examination, but you know that Jordan, in agreement with the states of the League, has plunged into the turmoil of the Zionist strife in order to crush the power of the Zionists, and strives to emerge from the affair with as few losses as possible; you will remember that I told you this at lunch during your first visit to me.

But while we in Transjordan[9] have been carrying on our military campaign and bearing the heaviest of military burdens alone, the League decides to set up in Gaza a feeble state for all Palestine[10] in order to get rid of its responsibilities, as is commonly said. This action means the acceptance and execution of partition. For my part, I shall not cease to rely on God in carrying out my duty. When I saw the Arab armies in Egypt to the west and in Syria and Lebanon to the north preparing and proceeding to carry out this plan and then failing to send in even a brigade, showing neither sympathy nor regard for the uprooted people of Palestine but continuing their useless incitement of them and expecting one state to carry out the conquest of Palestine, I kept my place in the vanguard as I had always determined to do.

Winter is approaching and the refugees are without shelter. The responsibility for them and for failing to settle the affair rests on those Arab states which instead of putting forth a military effort looked idly on. The deeds and steadfastness of my army are sufficient to disprove the slanders that have been fabricated against it.

My greetings to you and to all your brethren.

'Abdallah ibn al-Husayn

Amman, 30 September 1948

[9] The author uses the terms Jordan (al-Urdunn) and Transjordan (Sharq al-Urdunn) interchangeably.
[10] This refers to the so-called "Gaza Government" or "Government of All Palestine" set up by the Arab Higher Executive under Arab League auspices at Gaza in September 1948. Hajj Amin al-Husayni had been elected president of its assembly.

The demand for the internationalization of Jerusalem was the strangest and most unbalanced of the Arab national aims. It was one that disregarded the Arab rights and interests by handing the Holy Places over to international control and wrenching Jerusalem from the possession of the Arabs. It was my duty to stand resolutely and firmly in the defence of the Arab character of the Holy City and resist internationalization in all its aspects.

Opposition to the unity of both banks of the Jordan is solely the creation of the Arab Higher Executive, which is motivated by its own ends and which has no experience in politics or national defence, and no responsibility to guide it in internal and external affairs. His Excellency Tawfiq Pasha Abu al-Huda, president of the Jordanian Senate, on Monday, 24 April 1950[11] made clear in his speech in Parliament the degree of agreement which existed between him – he was Prime Minister at the time – and the responsible parties in the Arab governments concerning the question of incorporating this part of Palestine into our Hashimite Kingdom of the Jordan. In so doing we kept the remainder of Palestine from falling into the hands of the Jews. I shall reproduce below my first address, which was read before the united Parliament; the ensuing historic unanimous resolution made by Parliament regarding the unity of the two banks of the Jordan; the text of the resolution as ratified by me; and the reply of Parliament to my address.

Speech from the Throne
In the name of God the Merciful, the Compassionate!
Honourable Senators and Deputies:[12]

It is a cause of rejoicing that for the first time in the history of Jordan's constitutional life I open the session of Parliament with both banks of the Jordan united by the will of one people, one homeland, and one hope. It is a blessed step which the two banks have taken toward unity and upon the execution of which the sovereign people have entered. It has been made possible by the ethnic oneness of the people, by their patriotic pride and by their common interests. Jordan is like a bird with its wings spread east and west; it is its natural right to be united into a whole and for its people to join each other.

Senators and Deputies of the nation, you are well aware that the unity of

[11] This is the date on which the unification of both banks of the Jordan was announced.
[12] Directly following this is an invocation of blessings upon the Prophet, his family, and his companions, which has been omitted from this translation.

the two banks is an ethnic and actual reality. Its ethnic reality is established by their interlocking origins and ramifications, by the integration of their vital interests and the identity of their tribulations and their hopes. Its actual reality is established by the prevalence of firm ties of union between the two banks since 1922, or for the past twenty-eight years. These manifest and important ties – which include a common currency, joint defence, a share in port facilities, the stabilization of frontier security, the facilitation of customs and travel on the basis of common interests, and educational and legislative exchange—are among those factors which have given each of the two banks a privileged and special position in the eyes of the other.

Therefore, when Great Britain renounced its mandate over a Palestine cut off from the fatherland and the tempests of the Arab–Zionist strife began to blow, there was no alternative but to defend the rights of the Arabs and repel aggression by means of general Arab co-operation. The conflicting points of view which arose after the permanent armistice were due to a disregard of the real Jordan–Palestine situation; this disregard had been caused by a certain type of propaganda and conditioning which my government has continued to combat with wisdom, patience, a friendly spirit, trust, complete frankness, and strict good faith, whether in the Arab League Council or in private communications to its sister Arab states. In so doing my government has assumed that the Arabs possess sufficient sound instinct, perception, and zeal to push aside the obstacles and restore everything to its proper place. My government considers that the decision promulgated by the Arab League Political Committee on 12 April 1948[13] no longer stands, since the Arab states have agreed to the permanent armistice and have followed this with an acceptance of the United Nations' decisions on partition in contradiction to the aforementioned stand of the Political Committee.

However much I may welcome the idea of collective security and economic co-operation between the Arab states on sound bases, . . . I believe that there can be no security for any Arab people except after they have become genuinely united and after their scattered components have been reassembled whenever such action may be possible, in conformity with the general will, and not inconsistent with any existing undertaking or covenant. Unity, indeed, was the first objective of the Arab Revolt; nay, it was the mainstay of independence and the instrument by which the struggle was carried on. He who shrinks from it shrinks from his own nature and from the basis of his power. The position of Jordan and

[13] This decision ruled that the Arab armies were entering Palestine only to rescue it and not to occupy it; after liberation the country was to have been handed over to the owners to be governed as they wished.

14

Palestine demands that these two entities enjoy unity, which is the basis of their economic life, of the defence of their far-flung front lines and of the vital living-space of their Arab inhabitants since most ancient times. The pacts which the Arabs have made among themselves make it incumbent upon this unified entity to strengthen itself in every way made possible by its way of life, its self-esteem, its honour, and the realization of its legitimate aspirations.

Honourable Senators and Deputies.

It is a source of genuine satisfaction to me that our nation has not lost faith in the spirit of God and that events have added to its lustre and to its faith in itself. The full participation of the people on both banks of the Jordan in the general parliamentary elections is an indication that they feel themselves to be a single entity. They have been polled and they have collectively confirmed their essential unity, comprehending the deleterious material and moral effects of indefinitely-continued fragmentation and differing administration and legislation – following the acceptance of the permanent armistice – on the common homeland; this is what only the people of the land and its legal possessors can feel. Therefore, even though a final settlement realizing the right of the Arabs with regard to Palestine has not been attained, the confirmation of this unification, which has been accomplished in fact by the meeting of this esteemed assembly representing both banks of the Jordan, will materially strengthen this united nation's defence of the justice of its cause. My government will continue to defend the rights of the Arabs and the country's aspirations in the final settlement. It will endeavour, insofar as it is able, to lay the groundwork for full co-operation with its sister Arab states in all matters supporting these rights and aspirations. At the same time it will give due consideration to the value of peace, which unless accompanied by confidence and trust will be of little use in restoring the supremacy of right and the resumption of international relations on the basis of justice, integrity, and the fulfilment of covenants.

Honourable Senators and Deputies:

My government has announced with respect to its foreign policy that it will pursue amicable relations with all friendly states. In its internal programme it will have as its aim the modification of the constitution, as already promised, on the basis of parliamentary and ministerial responsibility and the preservation of the balance between the legislative, the executive, and the judicial powers. In execution of this, steps will be taken in this session toward the establishment of a special committee of experts and competent jurists to draw up a project for modification of the constitution not only along the most modern lines but also with a view to its suitability to the country's interests. My government at this very moment is working on the unification of the laws and on desirable reforms in the educational, administrative, and economic fields. It is urgently endeavouring also to provide employment, improve agricultural facilities, and in particular to bolster up the country's economy, while at the same time giving due attention to the refugee question with the aim of providing employment for refugees and preserving their self-respect. Two bills will be presented to your esteemed assembly in this extraordinary session for consideration and approval according to constitutional procedure: one dealing with the unification of both banks of the Jordan and the other with the annual budget for 1950–1951.

I therefore, in the name of High and Mighty God, declare this extraordinary session of the nation's new parliament to be open and I invite you to enter upon your labours. May God guide your steps and grant you and me success through His favour and grace. Amen.

The Historic Decree on the Unification of the Two Banks

In confirmation of the confidence of the nation; in acknowledgement of the meritorious efforts exerted by His Majesty 'Abdallah ibn al-Husayn, King of the Hashimite Kingdom of the Jordan, on behalf of the realization of the aspirations of the people; in reliance on the right of self-determination; in view of the present situation of the eastern and western banks of the Jordan and their ethnic, cultural, and geographic unity; and in consideration of the compulsion of their common interests and living space, the Jordanian Parliament representing both banks does on this 7th day of Rajab 1369, corresponding to 24 April 1950, declare as follows:

Firstly: It confirms the complete unity of the eastern and the western banks of the Jordan and their merging into one state, the Hashimite Kingdom of the Jordan, at the head of which is His Hashimite Majesty the exalted King 'Abdallah ibn al-Husayn, a state based on a parliamentary, constitutional regime and on equality of rights and duties among all its citizens.

Secondly: It confirms the reservation of all Arab rights in Palestine, the defence of such rights by all legitimate means and with full competence, without prejudice to the final settlement of their just case within the scope of the people's aspirations and of Arab co-operation and international justice.

Thirdly: This decree, issued by the two chambers of Parliament – the Senate and the Chamber of Deputies – representing both banks of the Jordan, shall be submitted to His Exalted Majesty and shall be considered effective upon receiving the high royal sanction.

Fourthly: This decree shall be published and executed by the government of the Hashimite Kingdom of the Jordan as soon as it has received high royal sanction and shall be communicated to our sister Arab states and to friendly foreign states by the usual diplomatic means.

Reply of the Senate
Your Majesty:

The Senate renders thanks to God for the foundation which He has been pleased to lay for unity and for His granting the wish of those who have prayed for this unification by His uniting the western bank of the Jordan with its sister eastern bank and joining them together in one kingdom under the redeeming Hashimite crown. This unity has been but the echo of a popular will and a patriotic desire. It has been a protection from calamities, and experience has taught us how great they can be. If this unification had taken place earlier, and if the people had possessed the necessary boldness to bring it about, the Arabs would have avoided their present fate. The Senate feels that it should thank His Exalted Majesty, experienced helmsman of the ship of state, for the discerning influence and penetrating perception that have found a way for the vessel amid violent tempests, passions, and partisan feelings.

The Senate tenders His Hashimite Majesty its most sincere thanks, admiration, and respect for the excellent spirit revealed in His Majesty's (may God support him!) earnest desire that the decision for unification should not prejudice any final settlement of the Palestine problem which might redound to the benefit and honour of the Arabs, and for his desire to co-operate with the Arab states within the scope of the people's aspirations. The Senate recalls also with much pride and gratitude His Majesty's (may God preserve him!) promise to modify the constitution, with the confidence that the anticipated modifications will produce changes conforming to social needs and will lay out the right way for the attainment of the nation's goals. Our body accepts with wholehearted support the straightforward policy and judicious plans set forth in the high Speech from the Throne as both clearly discerning the situation and courageously facing realities.

Your Majesty:

With reference to Your Majesty's statements and particularly your gracious Speech from the Throne, the Senate feels that it is its duty to speak of your solicitude and concern for the welfare of the refugees, your search for a way out from their difficulties, and your labours to assist them insofar as possible in returning to their homes and securing the restoration of their property. Therefore, the Senate believes that our country is in great need of the accomplishment of His Hashimite Majesty's wishes through the creation of a general economic, educational, and social renaissance in order that the country may stand on its own feet and not be a burden on itself or others. It is of the first importance that efforts be made to bring about this renaissance in order to realize both the short and the long-range economic and developmental aims of the country.

The Senate once again expresses its thanks to His Hashimite Majesty for his determination to follow this programme for encouraging solidarity and mutual tolerance. In so doing it hopes that the day may come when the Arabs will feel that, after having been dying and scattered remnants, they have experienced a renaissance through unity which has restored their self-respect. Your success in completing the reuniting of the scattered remnants of the Arab people and in continuing along the way you have chosen is in the hands of God; it is His to preserve you as a refuge and mainstay for the country and as a rallying-point and fortress for the Arabs.

Reply of the Chamber of Deputies
Your Majesty:

We, the Deputies of the nation representing both the western and the eastern banks of the kingdom, gathered for the first time in one assembly under one crown, have heard with pride and rejoicing the august Speech from the Throne. We have the honour to present to His Majesty our beloved King our sincere thanks and express our great indebtedness for the august royal felicitation on the people's confidence in us and for the gracious royal welcome to us in the new Parliament.

Your Majesty:

Our chamber is indeed proud to have the honour of ratifying the first decree unifying two sister countries under the leadership of Your Majesty. It is our hope that this blessed step will open a new era in the life of the Arab nation and that it will be an auspicious omen of the realization of our aims and aspirations to unity, sovereignty, and independence.

It is a cause of satisfaction and confidence that this unification has been brought about without any prejudice to the general Arab rights in Palestine or to the final settlement of their case. This unification, in fact, strengthens the defence of the justice of their cause and is a stimulus for the redoubling of efforts to arrive at a just solution which will preserve their rights and self-respect in co-operation with our sister Arab states.

Your Majesty:

We welcome the idea of collective security among the Arab states along with any step these states may take toward rapprochement, co-operation, and agreement among themselves. This collective security, however, should in no wise influence adversely the desire of the Arab peoples to unite and assemble their scattered members into a true unity founded on the free will of the people and within the limits of the common Arab interest.

18

Your Majesty:

It is a source of happiness and rejoicing to us, the Deputies of the nation, that Your Majesty has been pleased to carry out the will of your loyal people and through the agency of the Parliament grant them their full constitutional rights to make their laws and bear responsibility. In this manner there has been established the supremacy of the law, the independence of the judiciary, and the regulation of relations between the legislative and executive powers based on the responsibility of the ministers to Parliament.

Your Majesty has manifested gracious royal sympathy in being pleased urgently to further this desire, which is the aspiration of every Jordanian, and to order that necessary measures be taken in this session to constitute a special committee of experts and competent jurists to draft modifications of the constitution along the most modern and complete lines. They are aware that the Parliament should be represented on this committee in order to facilitate the execution of the august royal will.

Your Majesty:

Despite the calamities that have befallen us in Palestine and the disasters and upheavals that have afflicted our Arab homeland, we have not despaired of the possibility of a new renaissance for this nation. The rejection of the spirit of despair and defeat which Your Majesty has been pleased to manifest is indeed the strongest factor reassuring your people and encouraging them to push forward under Your Majesty's wise leadership toward the realization of the nation's goals and the people's hopes. We return to Your Majesty our deepest thanks for your fatherly sympathy towards the refugees and your efforts to rescue them from despair, hardship, and the poverty of their life.

Your Majesty:

Since we place our hopes in anticipated reforms in the fields of education, administration, and economic affairs, we reaffirm our desire that in educational reform there be followed a course of setting up the educational programme on sound, popular principles which are in harmony with the spirit of the times and which will introduce vocational education in the most widespread and beneficial manner.

We desire also that economic reform be based, insofar as possible, on a balance between exports and imports and that to this end national production should be increased and imports restricted as far as may be consistent with the country's interests. It is our hope that such reform will accept the principle of graduated taxation and of raising the standard of living of the fellah and the worker. We hope also that, to the degree possible, an effort will be made to draw up just social legislation to regulate labour conditions and safeguard the rights of the worker. With respect to administrative reform, it is our desire that the aim should be to serve the people and protect their interests. It should be carried out with regard for the rights of our fellow-citizens and should protect their freedoms, while at the same time paying due attention to technical competence and considerations peculiar to public office.

In closing, Your Majesty, we beseech God (may He be exalted and glorified!) to preserve you as a resource for Arabism and to strengthen us, under the protection of Your Majesty, for the service of the nation and the homeland.

It is apparent from the foregoing that in truth the Palestine problem is one of ignorance, obstinacy, and self-seeking on the part of persons who have throttled their homeland until they have almost completely destroyed its patriotic spirit. I bear witness to this before God and know that His anger will be mighty. But I am not of those who will be embarrassed before God and the tribunal of justice by any accusations made against me.

Some Events and Military Operations in Palestine

I have already said that it is not seemly for me to go into certain confidential matters which should be kept hidden in the interest of the Arabs and of Arab brotherhood, for the right to do so belongs to the Arab states as a whole. It is not for one party to discuss what concerns all of them.

Nevertheless it is my right to acquaint Arab public opinion in this chapter with matters which can be discussed openly. Among these are my relations with His Excellency Shukri al-Quwwatli and the events that transpired in Lydda and al-Ramlah, the happenings in Beersheba, the Egyptian withdrawal, the armistice at Rhodes, and the Triangle question. I believe that I have every right to speak about these subjects. Furthermore, with regard to the inter-nationalization of Jerusalem I shall discuss matters which should not be left unmentioned, because of the high place this Holy City occupies in the eyes of Islam. It holds a special position for every Muslim nation because of the Arab, Kurdish, Circassian, and Turkish blood which has been shed on its behalf throughout the history of Islam.

I shall begin, therefore, with the telephone conversation that took place between Damascus and Amman after the initial happenings of 15 May [1948]. Damascus had called Amman, saying that it was doing so because of certain thoughts which President al-Quwwatli (who at the time was being visited by Arab League Secretary

General 'Azzam Pasha) wished to express. The message referred to the necessity of refraining from advancing into Palestine and of providing the Palestinians with all possible arms and funds, and promised that if the Arab uprising actually got under way and needed effective assistance such aid would then be given.

Because of 'Azzam Pasha's presence in Damascus I was not sure at the time whether this really had been suggested to Damascus by Egypt or whether it was due to some distrust of me which had arisen in their minds and aroused a desire to discover my true intentions. At any rate, it was a moment that touched my soul with apprehension and anxiety, for the Arab Legion was engaged in a violent struggle for Jerusalem and had advanced to the coastal plain in the vicinity of Bab al-Wad, Lydda, and al-Ramlah on one hand, and Tulkarm and al-'Affulah on the other. My answer was a flat rejection of this strange proposal and I requested to speak to the Secretary General of the League himself, who protested that my suspicions were entirely unfounded. They naturally agreed with me immediately as to the necessity of persevering in our course, but added by way of excuse that the state of preparation did not permit assistance to other fronts. As a consequence, the Syrian forces were stalled around Samakh and defeated at Safad and Nazareth. The Lebanese forces took nothing but defensive action and even lost some Lebanese villages.

As a result of this the situation of the command compelled real co-operation between the Iraqi and the Jordanian forces and demanded that they be considered as complementary to each other. I kept a unit on the left of the Syrian forces and moved the Iraqis from around al-Mafraq to Amman and by way of Jisr Damiyah and Allenby Bridge to Nablus. The arrival of these troops saved Janin and the whole Triangle from the gravest danger. Then, supporting each other, they gradually advanced until they reached Ra's al-'Ayn, where they faced the large Jewish colonies with the red sand dunes behind them.

I pushed the fighting Jordanians into Lydda and al-Ramlah, awaiting the Egyptian Army's advance from the coast to Jaffa. It had been expected that the Egyptians would finish off the Jewish colonies in the whole of the Negev, but nothing of the sort ever happened. Instead, there was delay and stalling, a concealing of the true course of events, a failure to inform me of the correct number of Egyptian brigades, battalions, volunteers, and others which 'Azzam Pasha had brought up and committed to the Hebron–Bethlehem front and which had established contact with the Arab

Legion in the Jerusalem area. I was not even allowed to inspect these troops as commander of the united forces, which I began to be in name only.

Even more underhanded was the confiscation of a ship loaded with arms and ammunition which had left Suez for al-'Aqabah. It was seized by Egyptian naval forces, taken back to Suez, and unloaded despite my protests and persistent entreaties to His Majesty King Faruq and the Egyptian Government. My last hope of regaining this material disappeared when I was told that it had been distributed among the Egyptian forces, which I considered a case of robbing Peter to pay Paul. The result of this loss was that when the first cease-fire took place[14] the Arab Legion possessed ammunition and heavy weapons sufficient for only two days' fighting.

During this armistice period I went to Egypt and stated my case. When I asked the late al-Nuqrashi Pasha what Egypt's intentions were, he assured me that Egypt was loyal to the cause and that it would persevere in the struggle until complete success was won. I also expressed to the Palace my desire to visit the headquarters of the Egyptian supreme command in Palestine in my capacity as Commander in Chief, but it was indicated that this would not be fitting since His Majesty had not yet visited the front himself. Thereupon I suggested the necessity of His Majesty's visiting Jerusalem, but was told that flying would be dangerous. When I replied that it would be possible to do so via the Suez al-'Aqabah–Amman route, other excuses were brought forth. If this visit had taken place it would have been a successful move which would have resulted in our taking all of Jerusalem through an attack by the three royal armies in the presence of the Regent of Iraq ('Abd al-Ilah), His Majesty King Faruq, and myself. Thus I succeeded neither in securing the return of the confiscated ammunition nor in seizing the greatest opportunity of the war by employing the full strength of the united command. I was unsuccessful also in getting His Majesty to carry out the objective of the command, since the forces of the four states for all practical purposes were not under the command of the Deputy Commander in Chief, Brigadier Nur al-Din Mahmud Pasha, who was commander of the Iraqi forces and responsible for all troops.

Following this I went to Najd while the Arab League was in session in Egypt and left orders with my then Prime Minister, Tawfiq Pasha Abu al-Huda, that under no circumstances should the first armistice be broken, even though the government should have

[14] 11 June 1948.

to resign, until the army had obtained the light and heavy material it needed. Unfortunately, I was informed of the rupture of the armistice by Sayyid Pachachi[15] when I arrived in Baghdad on my return from al-Riyad. This breach, which was the cause of indescribable distress and worry to me, resulted in the Jewish movements against Lydda and al-Ramlah which caused the Iraqi and the Jordanian commands to hold back, since they were meeting a general attack with insufficient material. We conserved what we had in order to repulse enemy attacks from whatever quarter they might come.

This was the most glaring example of the Arab League's mishandling of affairs and of the consequences which the member states had to suffer as a result of its mistaken and ineffectual policy.

When the second cease-fire was declared[16] it was soon broken by Israel's surprise attack on the Egyptian forces in the Negev in the area of al-Falujah and Beersheba. The Egyptian forces were split, enabling the Israelis to penetrate between al-Falujah and Beersheba and between Beersheba and Gaza, thus cutting the various units of the Egyptian Army off from one another. Strangely enough, when this took place the united command was not informed of what had happened. Instead, the Secretary General of the Arab League publicly broadcast the necessity of the Arab forces' coming to the rescue from all directions to save the situation.

In the meantime, the late Prime Minister al-Nuqrashi Pasha of Egypt, Syrian Prime Minister Jamil Mardam Bey, and Husni Bey al-Za'im[17] had come to Amman, where His Royal Highness the Regent of Iraq and Iraqi Chief of Staff General Salih Sa'ib Pasha were already present. On the night we all met in council over five minutes passed before anyone spoke a word. The Regent motioned me to begin the conversation, but it was difficult for me to say anything in view of what had happened to the Egyptian Army. Therefore, directing my words to al-Nuqrashi Pasha, I said, "Let us hear what His Excellency has to say." His reply, word for word, was, "God! I have come to listen, not to talk." I answered, "I think that Your Excellency should do the talking under the present circumstances in view of the fact that Beersheba has been lost and al-Falujah is besieged." "Who said so?" he queried. "The Egyptian forces are still holding their positions." "Perhaps," I countered,

[15] Muzahim al-Pachachi, Prime Minister of Iraq from June 1948 to January 1949.
[16] 18 July 1948.
[17] Later to become the military dictator of Syria. The meetings described here took place on 12–13 July 1948.

"the news has not yet reached the ears of Your Excellency. I had thought that you would point out the necessity of military help, as desired by the Egyptian command, in order to save the situation." "No," he said, "the Egyptian Government has no need of anyone's assistance. But where are the royal Jordanian and Iraqi forces? And we all know that the Syrian forces are useless." This was said in the presence of Jamil Mardam Bey, who was listening. "I take it then," I replied, "that Your Excellency has come here to accuse us. You have just said that the Egyptian Government seeks help from no one, but 'Azzam Pasha is broadcasting cries for help. Are you heaping scorn on the Arabs in their own house – the house in which Jordan, Iraq, Syria, and Lebanon are gathered?" "I seek forgiveness of God," he said, "I have not come to accuse anyone."

At this point Salih Sa'ib Pasha said that when news of the Jewish attack reached him he inquired of the Egyptian headquarters in al-Zarqa as to the truth of the report, but had not succeeded in obtaining an answer in spite of repeated verbal and written requests. Under such circumstances it was not considered possible to move without a clarification of the situation. Thereupon I interjected, "What you are saying is true. I am going to perform my evening prayers while you talk."

So I left them, apprehensive of the result of this verbal tension. When I returned I found that they had discussed the All-Palestine Government[18] and the necessity of my accepting and recognizing it. This I vigorously refused to do, because I knew that it was ill-advised and I was convinced that those participating in it were incompetent. Jamil Mardam Bey took a true Arab stand when he joined me in refusing to hear of this imaginary government or to believe that any good could come of it.

The meeting then broke up and reconvened later at the Egyptian Legation, where al-Nuqrashi Pasha admitted that Beersheba had fallen. The following evening the same personages met at the home of al-Nuqrashi Pasha's host in Amman, Isma'il Pasha al-Bilbaysi. Here it was agreed that the Egyptian Army should be supported by two movements: one by the Iraqi and Jordanian armies from the south and the other in conjunction with the Syrian forces from the centre and the north. On this note the meeting broke up at midnight, and it was decided that General Salih Sa'ib Pasha and Colonel Husni al-Za'im should make the necessary arrangements for carrying out this plan. Nevertheless, hardly had the next day dawned when they met again and al-Nuqrashi Pasha told them to

<hr>

[18] See above, note 10.

disregard the previous night's decision, since the need had passed. Certain units of the Jordanian forces in Jerusalem and Bab al-Wad, however, had already moved down to al-Dahiriyah and Bayt Jibrin; they saved the situation on the Hebron front and the Egyptian forces pulled back from Bayt Jibrin to Hebron. In addition to this, the Egyptian forces in al-Falujah were receiving their supplies through the Arab Legion until they were rescued.

These are some of the matters which I believe should be made known at the present time.

Between Syria and Jordan

It would not be fitting for me to complete my memoirs without discussing the subject of divided Syria, for unless its people keep to the true road toward their goal there can be no security for the Arabs.

This land suffered sore afflictions after its conquest by General Gouraud,[19] and there was no rapprochement between France and Syria or stability in their relations. With World War II the independent Syrian Republic was born, only to undergo another period of trial under Husni al-Za'im; it is true that needed changes were made, but he (may God forgive him!) likewise put himself before his country. Furthermore, I recall that when the Jordanian Government sent the most recent Syrian government the expression of its most fervent hopes for a meeting which might result in an exchange of diplomatic representatives and in the conclusion of an agreement of *bon voisinage* and brotherhood like that existing between Jordan and Iraq, the chief of the Syrian Government made excuses and did not receive the representative of the Jordanian Government. Perhaps some other Arab quarter or quarters exerts influence in this direction on every Syrian government which inclined toward its natural state of unity and strength. It is no secret that if I set this down in writing it is because of the responsibility I feel as the one surviving leader of the revolt for liberation from Ottoman Turkey.

On 16 November 1950 I left Iraq on my way back to Jordan, grieving for Her Majesty the mother of Faysal II,[20] may God have mercy on her. Among the strange things I had heard in Iraq was the

[19] Leader of the French forces which drove Faysal from Damascus in July 1920.

[20] The reference is to Queen Mother 'Aliyah, wife of the late King Ghazi, who at this time was gravely ill. She died on 22 December 1950.

accusation that certain Syrians in the service of His Majesty King 'Abd al-'Aziz ibn Sa'ud had brought in funds to be used for the assassination of designated political personalities in Syria and that the attempt on the life of Colonel al-Shishakli was the work of this group.[21] Another item was that Nash'at Shaykh al-Ard,[22] the brother of King 'Abd al-'Aziz's physician, had paid a certain person to murder me. I had seen similar things done by the Ottoman Committee of Union and Progress; when it wanted to get rid of anyone it used to incite someone to kill him, after which the Committee cast suspicion on one of its own enemies in order to stir up dissension and divert suspicion from itself.

I had not the slightest doubt that King 'Abd al-'Aziz never ordered such a thing. But it is possible that Shaykh al-Ard used certain monies to carry out his designs against me or others whom he and his confederates might have wanted to put out of the way as a service to a certain Syrian personage who had either ordered or instigated them to do it. It had already happened that the political leader Dr 'Abd al-Rahman al-Shahbandar had been murdered by a well-known political clique.[23] Treachery and assassination are the basest characteristics of cowards and are not the mark of men who do not drive themselves to the depths of dishonour. Glory be to God! How Syria has fallen into vain and murderous hands which have committed deeds that make one shudder! They have betrayed each other and each has perished in turn. This al-Shishakli cannot travel about or even sleep without protection, but unless God saves him he will meet his death at the hands of his own bodyguard. For just as the blood of al-Shahbandar removed Shukri al-Quwwatli from his seat and exiled Jamil Mardam from his country, so will the ambitious and the treacherous ensnare the present rulers of Syria in their trickery.

Syria today is in a dangerous situation, for the United Nations both forbids aggression and at the same time permits it. Syria is a country which political pulling and hauling divided up into four parts following World War I. When God put an end to the mandates as a result of World War II, the division of that country was maintained by those of its self-seeking and ambitious sons who are now murdering each other. Although this is aggression, it is

[21] The attempt took place on 11 October 1950.

[22] He was indicted by a Syrian military court on 11 November 1950. Cf. *The Middle East Journal*, vol. 5, no. 1 (Winter 1951), p. 87 under 12 November.

[23] In July 1940. See A. H. Hourani, *Syria and Lebanon*, London, New York, and Toronto, 1946, p. 234.

permitted by the United Nations. If the remaining parts of the homeland had desired to correct such a state of affairs by united and fruitful perseverance, this would have been opposed as aggression also. But there must be an end to every situation, and this evil state of affairs will terminate in a unity which will bind up the wound and by God's will banish these arrogant spreaders of corruption.

In the face of this situation it is incumbent upon me once again to remind the Arabs of their duty to practise self-denial and preserve the interests of the homeland by giving the best men precedence over the worst and avoiding that which will disappoint and disunite them.

The Arabs must now free themselves from those Arabs who have managed to obtain control of them. This is apparent from a brief glance at what has been taking place in Syria since the end of Shukri al-Quwwatli's regime:[24] the excesses of Husni al-Za'im, his assassination[25] and the confusion that followed it; the killing of Lieutenant Colonel Muhammad al-Nasir,[26] commanding officer of the air force; the al-Hinnawi débâcle[27] and the armed attack on al-Shishakli;[28] the closing of the Syro–Jordanian and the Syro–Iraqi borders for purposes of search; the imprisonment of certain prominent men, including a former Minister of Defence[29] (who is now said to be on the point of death as the result of a hunger strike); the investigation of the army which is now taking place in Egypt; and the uproar attending various other questions. My conclusion from all this is that the Arabs must give up day-dreaming and apply themselves to realities.

Syria and Iraq are respectively the western and the eastern frontiers of the Arab lands. Syria lies on the Mediterranean coast and is bounded on the north by Turkey. Iraq, on the eastern frontier, is bounded on the east by Iran and on the south by the Persian Gulf. As I have already said, these two countries are contiguous to large states, lie at the eastern extremity of the Mediterranean, and form an important political and geographic unity. To the south of them are the deserts of Najd and the Hijaz and the land which its inhabitants

[24] As a result of the al-Za'im *coup* of 30–31 March 1949.

[25] By the al-Hinnawi *coup* forces on 14 August 1949.

[26] 1 August 1950.

[27] He was arrested by the al-Shishakli *coup* forces on 19 December 1949. After his release he retired to Beirut, where he was assassinated on 30 October 1950. The assassin was a cousin of Muhsin al-Barazi, liquidated by al-Hinnawi at the time of his *coup*.

[28] 11 October 1950.

[29] Ahmad al-Sharabati, arrested on 17 October 1950.

call *al-mustaswirah*: that which receives the rain remaining after other lands have been watered; it is barren and subject to famine every two or three years.

If there is anything that wounds the soul it is the advances made to Syria by two well-known states of the Arab League[30] and the continual visits of responsible parties in Syria to these two countries in order to receive directions, instructions, and support. All this has affected both the visitors and the visited. It hurts the soul of every man who took part in the original Arab revolt and the separation of the Arabs from the Ottoman state to see that the Arabs have not chosen from among themselves men who would safeguard their honour and lead them back to their former glory.

These are painful things. I should not be wrong if I should describe them as the elegy of the Arab people.

Minutes of the meeting held in Raghadan Palace[31] on Tuesday, 28 November 1950 by His Hashimite Majesty King 'Abdallah; H. E. Dr Nazim al-Qudsi, Prime Minister of Syria; and H. E. Colonel Fawzi Silu, Syrian Minister of Defence.

His Majesty the King opened the meeting with the following words:

I have read the letter of His Excellency the President of Syria which Your Excellency has brought and I have found that it contains the essence of the mutual support, brotherhood, and assistance toward which we must work. I trust that you will succeed in the many matters on which you are to confer with the Jordanian government, beginning with the question of the exchange of diplomatic representation, and that you will turn your attention toward abolishing the estrangement between us which exists at present. For we are one country and are brothers and neighbours. Before you begin these conversations I should like to review for you the situation in both its former and its present aspects.

You are aware that I am the sole survivor of those who raised the revolt against the Ottomans. The Arabs possessed national demands for the realization of which we had worked since the proclamation of the Turkish constitution of 1908. The movement for obtaining these demands was headed by Syrian organizations whose object was to bring about the decentralization of the administration. These organizations gained much ground and almost succeeded. You recall how the late Sheikh 'Abd al-Hamid al-Zahrawi was called to Paris to meet the Turkish Minister of

[30] The reference is to Egypt and Saudi Arabia.
[31] In Amman.

the Interior Tal'at Bey,[32] with regard to the demand for a decentralized administration for Syria; and how al-Sayyid al-Idrisi was granted his demands in southern and western 'Asir. You will recall also that the Ottoman state recognized the Imam Yahya Hamid al-Din as Imam of the Zaydis[33] with the title of Commander of the Believers.

Then there occurred the assassination of the Crown Prince of Austria at Sarajevo, which led to World War I. At that time my brother Faysal and I were in Istanbul as deputies from Jidda and Mecca respectively. We saw that the Turks had shifted their position and, abandoning their old friends, had decided to side with the enemies of Russia. Their object in so doing was to prevent all non-Turkish elements from pressing for decentralization and from making other demands. Instead of attempting to conceal these aims they informed us and the deputies to Parliament of what they intended to do. At first they expressed good intentions toward us, but as time passed it became clear that they had other ideas in mind.

I had not demanded a decentralized administration for Syria within its present boundaries, but for all of Syria from Tabuk in the south to the vilayets of Aleppo and Beirut and the *mutasarrifiyah* (governorate) of Jerusalem. Upon the outbreak of war the Turks seized the opportunity to decree the suppression of those elements which were seeking reform. They began to move the people from one place to another and to plunder and assault them. At this point the Arabs lost their patience, for they were in no mood to remain in a state of confusion until they had either exchanged one master for another or had been exterminated. Faysal was in Damascus with Jamal Pasha "the blood-shedder", ostensibly to raise troops or for some other important matter. There the members of the *Suriya al-Fatah* (Young Syria) Party met and resolved to raise a general revolt in order to create a single nation, state, and flag which would protect the honour of the East and restore its lost glory. My brother Faysal returned carrying the seals of the Syrian leaders in a pouch as proof of the sincerity of the promise they had made to each other to work for Arab independence.[34]

To make a long story short, I was commander of the Army of the East when the revolt began. I did not consider that I was fighting for the Hijaz alone, but for the defence of Syria, Iraq, Najd, the Yemen, and every other Arab land. With the helping hand of God we overcame difficulties and obstacles, and by the time Turkey collapsed our Arab army had reached

[32] Tal'at Bey (later Pasha) was himself of minority (Pomak) origin and a revolutionary. He was one of the principal leaders of the Young Turk Movement and an ardent Pan-Tauranist.

[33] A Shiite sect to which the ruling group in the Yemen belongs.

[34] See George Antonius, *The Arab Awakening*, London, 1938, pp. 152–3.

Aleppo. But hardly had the armistice been concluded when we began to hear strange rumours and talk that bewildered us. Britain began to advocate Iraq for the Iraqis and the serpents of separatism began to raise their heads. Many men's minds were changed and we fell into the evils of the mandates. France was in Syria and Lebanon, and Britain was in Iraq, Palestine, and Jordan.

After the collapse of Faysal's throne in Damascus I left the Hijaz for Ma'an to demand the due which had been taken from him. Continuing from there to Amman, I was called to Jerusalem to consult with Mr Winston Churchill, then British Colonial Secretary. When we met he said to me, "France will not tolerate Faysal's return to Syria. If you remain here, behave well, and pursue the right course in this matter both here and in the Hijaz, we hope that France may change its mind and after a few months give you your due; Syria will then be yours again." I asked him to give me time to consult the Syrians who had assembled in Amman, and they agreed that I should remain. However, when the attack on General Gouraud took place at al-Shajarah, France used the situation as an excuse to increase its tyranny and arrogance. Thus one thing led to another until the outbreak of the uprising which was centred in the Jabal Druze. In the meantime we, in our part of the land of Syria, constituted for the Syrians a place of refuge where they recovered their strength and found willing help and care for their wounds.

The various parties and political societies continued to appeal for unity and rejection of the partition of Syria, calling upon the Arabs to become one people under one state.

Following the defeat of France in World War II Syria attained its independence. It most grievously pains me, who revolted for Arab unity, to see those who participated in the revolt become not only supporters of partition, but even its most vigorous propagandists. The earlier national objective of complete national unity was transformed into one of an odious and harmful partition. I say frankly that we, the Hashimites, left the Hijaz for the sake of Syria and Palestine and lost it to a barbarous Arab people who set themselves with a will to destroying, plundering, and committing desecration in its holy territory. Not satisfied with inflicting this heavy loss on us, they consider everyone who comes to pay his respects to me as having committed a crime worthy of imprisonment and torture.

We of the Hashimite house were the prime factor in the Arabs' attainment to a place of honour. Their first age of glory was the creation of Muhammad (may God bless him and grant him peace!), and their second was the work of the creator of the Arab Revolt.[35] It is because of this that

[35] Sharif (later King) Husayn, father of King 'Abdallah.

some of you have become kings, princes, and presidents and have attained other high offices.

Now we see the Jews facing us across a long border – a thorn in our eye and in our side. It is strange that the Arab community continues to concentrate its efforts and hopes on the Arab League and hesitates to liquidate the present state of affairs within itself. The League is made up of men who do not study the true situation in the various Arab countries. In these countries cabinets come and go, but the League is headed by one man who always remains.[36] He directs its affairs in the interest of Egypt, his country, and appoints Egyptians to office for the purpose of realizing this one aim. To him Egypt is everything; he believes that the interests of the Arabs must be subordinated and the divisive tendencies among them encouraged for the benefit of Egypt. When I speak of all this and review the events that have happened my heart is filled with despair. Although I am the sole survivor of those who raised the Arab Revolt, who came to the help of the Arabs, who took revenge for our martyrs and resisted the designs of the Turks, I see my efforts thanklessly denied and repudiated for the sake of personal ambitions and the appeasement of partisan desires.

What have we done that our lands should be made subject to the whims of a person or state which heretofore has done nothing for the interests of the Arabs? We left our home to fight injustice and aggression, and we took our due and that of our countries by the edge of our swords. But others were appointed to lead us and they began openly to plot against the community of Arab states, of which they had never acknowledged that they were a part except when they found it in their interest to do so. This situation grows worse from day to day, and if it continues it will throw us into the arms of foreign powers. I do not believe that there is a single Arab who would want such a thing to come to pass.

Next door to us are the Jews, who constitute a permanent threat to us. They not only possess an army, an air force, and capital, but in addition are supported by the United States and most of Europe. Jordan is your homeland and its people are your people. I am only a simple Hijazi who serves the Arabs and is sacrificing himself for them. It is my relationship to the line of the Prophet that impels me to work for the unity of the Arabs. Thus my zeal for the glory of the Arabs is nothing new or of recent date as in the case of others.

Now the situation is in your hands. If you wish you can either raise the status of the Arabs or abase it. The Jews are an ever-present danger, more so than any Arab state; but I and my people are constantly on guard and we will not hesitate for a moment to carry out our duty to defend every foot of

[36] The reference is to 'Abd al-Rahman 'Azzam Pasha, Secretary General of the Arab League.

our soil. You are aware that there is an alliance between ourselves and the British, who have undertaken to defend our borders as they now stand after our integration of the eastern part of Palestine. We have the strength and the means, therefore, with which to defend ourselves. Our treaty with the British will be implemented if the Jews attack us, but I do not believe that this will happen since the Jews have no desire to stir up trouble the end of which they cannot foresee.

In the face of this danger we must reach an understanding which will permit all the segments of former undivided Syria to act together in order to work for the attainment of this factor of security. For I and the Jordanian Government and people consider ourselves a part of Syria, even though you may not.

As you have already said, we are primarily concerned with the exchange of diplomatic representation. We also want every Syrian to be assured that we will not fight against Syria, for whose sake we battled the Ottoman Turks, and will not compel it to do what it does not want to do. On my part, I am always ready to help Syria and I am willing to extend assistance to Syria as soon as it enjoys stability. After these problems have been liquidated there will be nothing to prevent our Prime Ministers and Ministers of Defence, Finance, Foreign Affairs, and so forth, from meeting to study the situation, and if they reach an agreement the Syrian community will be capable of repelling any aggression. So help your country and co-operate in that which will benefit it.

As for me, I am a simple Meccan and I repeat that I will not fight you in order to conquer your country. For how could I fight against you when I have fought for you? We want you to be as you wish to be, but the partition of former Syria worries me, since it is the source of all danger. I am afraid also that certain persons are uttering undeserved and unheard-of calumnies against me. They have already openly revealed their hostility and are determined to expel us from the Arab League, despite the fact that we are the pride of the Arabs and the fountainhead of their glory. Furthermore, they have opposed the national hopes of the Arabs by strongly advocating the internationalization of Jerusalem. Do they not know that internationalization will lead to the loss of the Holy City and Hebron and Nablus as well? Why, then, have they launched against us a widespread attack to help them gain their personal ends when we are the ones who strove and sacrificed to save for the Arabs that part of Palestine they still possess? Would they think better of us if we had let various bits of Palestine be swallowed up by others? You should visit these areas so that you can obtain an idea of the sacrifices which the Arab Legion has made for them and see the tremendous responsibilities which have been thrown upon its shoulders. Visit the refugees in their tents and the fellahin in their villages; ask those you meet about their condition. Go back to your country with the whole truth and speak it openly. These refugees are our brothers and every one of them is dear to us and to you.

After you have thoroughly studied the situation, then decide what you want to do to pick up the pieces and bring about the unification of Syria. You are perfectly free agents. If you choose a republic I shall not oppose it. If you believe that a confederation of independent states is preferable I shall accede to your wishes and strive to co-ordinate our efforts and actions whether in the field of finance or of foreign policy. I assure you that Iraq welcomes the proposals I have made. When this has been done we shall be able, in the event of war with communism, to ward off the danger and our country will not become a field of battle.

In bygone days Syria was a centre of the Fourth Ottoman Army and Iraq was a centre of the Fifth; these armies contained leaders from both countries. Therefore, since our country possesses strength it will be ruled by those who are well qualified. In this connection the battle of Palestine is an example and a lesson for us: we were prevented from attaining our objective only by the lack of arms and ammunition and by the absence of top administrators and a genuine unified command. God be praised, you lack neither knowledge nor understanding. You have military men and men of finance and you are the pride of the Arabs. But do I not see your ranks torn asunder and not a day passing without one of you being put to death or deprived of power? Even more strange is the fact that we see the states which gave assistance to your two late rulers hasten to support the slayer of the man they had previously helped and the instigator of the latest revolt.

As a Muslim and an Arab I cannot accept such a state of affairs. Shukri al-Quwwatli and I did not see eye to eye, but when Husni al-Za'im staged his *coup* I wrote to al-Quwwatli inviting him to come to Amman and set up a government here. Thereupon Egypt suddenly began to show an interest in Husni al-Za'im; it decorated him with the Order of Muhammad 'Ali and abandoned its former friend. Then Husni al-Za'im was killed and it was not long before Sami al-Hinnawi met the same end. May God guide mankind to the right path!

You are welcome among us; we are your brethren and that which you fear touches us as well as yourselves. I repeat what I have said regarding the necessity of your visiting the frontiers. My cabinet ministers are your brothers, so meet with them night and day and decide what will benefit this nation. May God grant you success! What you have heard from me is the word of a man whose experience and knowledge are the fruit of many years.

Dr al-Qudsi's Reply

I thank Your Majesty for this clear statement of and comprehensive commentary on the Arab cause. I thank you also for the counsel and advice which you have been pleased to give. I shall tell His Excellency the President of the Republic of Syria of the welcome and kindness we have found and I shall convey to him what Your Majesty has said.

Your Majesty, we are greatly desirous that the Arab kings should strive with their well-known wisdom to find a solution to the present situation and concern themselves with the future alone, for a return to the past will bring only evil and hateful consequences. I am convinced that the mistakes of the past have been due to many factors which are known to Your Majesty and which it is unnecessary to recount here.

Today we have a great hope, but we stand also in the presence of a great danger with which we must deal before it grows even more serious. There have been both successes and failures in the past, but these pale before greater successes and failures which may come to pass if we do not travel the right road and keep the interests of the Arabs in view. The world today is changing and peoples are marching ahead rapidly. We must not lag behind other nations, for these changes embrace ways of life, thought, and belief. For example, before World War II if a single Frenchman had said "We will not fight Russia," he would have been condemned to death; but today there are millions of Frenchmen who declare that they will not fight Russia and they have no fear of punishment. In the past it was kings, presidents, and politicians who ruled, but today the voice of the people must be listened to when it is a question of matters affecting them. It is on this basis that we hope that kings and presidents will deal with the present and the future, since there is no profit in concerning ourselves with the past.

We Syrians are being held up as an example of the differences which exist among the Arabs. One state says that we are in its camp, while another claims that we are on its side. What we have come to tell you is that we are working only for the interests of the Arabs and that we are not followers of any one party. Our sole desire is to pray God that He may unite our ranks and make us to speak with one voice. I have already told His Excellency your Minister of Foreign Affairs that the problem is a most serious one, for Palestine borders on Jordan, Syria, Lebanon, and Egypt, and the Jews know that if we were in agreement we should jointly be able to repel any aggression. For if they should launch an attack against us the three states would not be able to throw it back without the military co-operation of Egypt. Egypt, likewise, would be unable to repulse a Jewish attack without the military co-operation of these other three states. We want to rid ourselves of this continual threat, for what military expert believes that Egypt can be safe from the Jews unless it receives the co-operation of the Arabs?

I hope that we can leave our personal feelings aside, for the people have awakened and hate and rancour against us are being hatched among the new generation. I remember that in 1948 my nine-year-old son, who had been listening to the radio, called out to me: "You have deceived us enough! You claim that you have defeated the Jews, but from what has happened it seems that you are the ones who have been defeated!" Our children today have no trust in us and no confidence in our honesty.

As an Arab people we love all Arabs, but we must make our duty clear to others. Since you have the most experience, have followed the Arab cause, and have supported it from the beginning down to the present, I hope that you will establish contact with the Arab kings and with your high purpose and great ability endeavour to put an end to existing differences on which the Jews rely for their success. We should like to see you set a good example for your fellow kings. The evil which is before us is just as apparent to us Syrians as to you, but our present desire is to remove Syria from the field lest it become an arena of controversy. Let it not be said that we are partisans of this or that axis. We have our own duties to attend to; the development of our resources, the education of our children, and the treatment of our sick. Our heart is open to all Arabs, not to any one particular group to the exclusion of the others.

Comments by His Majesty

I have heard what you have just said, but I draw your attention to the incontrovertible truth that he who has no past has no future. He who forgets his past is like one who is just beginning his life; our past is a source of honour, not shame. The Arabs have their Koran, which even their present divided condition cannot cause us to forget.

The Jews were brought to Palestine and set about preparing themselves financially and militarily while those who were looking on were heedless of the danger they presented. We are all familiar with what happened after they had completed their preparations and the mandate had come to an end. The Jews would never have been able to accomplish this if the Arab states had possessed a unified command and a sincere determination. The month of May 1948 would have marked the end of the Jews as a community threatening the Arabs.

You have said that your hearts are open to all Arabs. Have you not heard the reports of your numerous compatriots who have visited Najd and the Hijaz regarding the anarchy and terrible oppression which prevails there? The Hijaz is suffering from the worst kind of humiliation and disgrace. As for Egypt, we know what Egypt is like from the disgraceful scandals revealed in its press which bring shame to every Arab. Egypt, a country of twenty million inhabitants, is more concerned with attacking other people than with countering Jewish attacks on us.

But we and Iraq have our eyes open to the attacks on us. Likewise, we both are pained by the hesitancy and the changes taking place in Syria, as well as by newspaper reports of party quarrels, assassinations, and lack of obedience to those who rule. It is these events that cause us to fear new movements which may change the situation and destroy both national feeling and morality. The present state of affairs is not a reassuring one, for Syria will be unable to ward off the Jews or any other nation. I trust that you do not forget where our borders lie, for if the Jews were to launch an attack against you, ourselves, or Lebanon, they would reach their objective before the Egyptians, the Najdis, or the Iraqis could come to our help.

Such being the case, the situation demands that we three take measures against the danger before its effects are felt. We, on our part, are ready and I beseech you to watch us night and day, for we are your brethren and we shall not divorce our past from our present or our future. You may be sure that I am prepared to extend help to you if you need it; I will not hesitate for a moment in my duty toward you for I am of you, with you, and for you.

Dr al-Qudsi: I hope, Your Majesty, that you are of the Arabs, with the Arabs, and for the Arabs. The Arab lands extend from the shores of the Atlantic to Iran, and in North Africa there are sixty million Arabs while in Arabia there are only nineteen million. We cannot forget our brethren in North Africa, for it was upon them that the glory of Andalusia was founded.

His Majesty: Do not forget, Your Excellency, that when Andalusia was conquered the centre of the caliphate was in Damascus. Medina, Damascus, and Baghdad were the centres of the caliphate; the rest were nothing more than colonies and mandates, to use modern political parlance. You must return to the past in order not to lose your future.

But with regard to the question of agreement between the kings and the elimination of the estrangement which you say has grown up among them, I may say that I forgot my enmity, disregarding my feelings, and paid visits to al-Riyad[37] and Cairo, but I do not believe that my journey to Najd produced any results.

Dr al-Qudsi: I believe, Your Majesty, that it did have some good effect.

His Majesty: How can Your Excellency say that was of any benefit when your judges and investigators have proved in official and public documents that those in Najd sent people and money to Syria in order to have me assassinated? Under such circumstances is it possible for anyone,

[37] King 'Abdallah arrived at al-Riyad on 27 June 1948.

however big-hearted, to have any friendship for a person who he knows wishes him nothing but evil and destruction?

Dr al-Qudsi: Your Majesty, no one denies your great service to the Arab cause and your long effort on behalf of Arab independence. But present circumstances require that Your Majesty make new sacrifices for the sake of conciliation and the ending of this estrangement, namely –

His Majesty: Have you reached your fortieth year of age?

Dr al-Qudsi: I am forty-five years old and was a child of eight when the Arab Revolt began.

His Majesty: At that time I was leading the Eastern Army of the Arab Revolt and was fighting the Ottomans in the defence of Najd, Iraq, the Yemen, Syria, and Lebanon. How could I forget the efforts which I made and the homeland in which the revolt broke out? I was driven from it by Bedouin who have no place in their hearts either for you or for Palestine. They have finished off their work in my native country by sending money to a band of mercenaries to murder me in this portion of the Arab homeland.

May God forgive what has happened in the past! You are welcome here and your visit will be returned by Sa'id Pasha.[38] Do whatever you think best for ourselves and yourselves. Our brethren in Iraq will welcome whatever we may agree upon; would that our Minister of Defence could visit every part of your cherished country!

At any rate I thank you; you are in your own country and among your own people.

Iraq: What Is Its Place in the Arab Community?

There is no darkness for him who can see; no gloom for him who has ability; no hesitation for him who is endowed with perception; and no fear for him who knows the truth and speaks it. This much is true.

You will not be surprised, therefore, if I say that Iraq and its people, both Sunnis and Shiites, trust in the Prophet's house[39] – the heart which beats for them and the land which has paid them homage and to which they in turn pay homage. The wealth of Iraq was created from the blood of the members of the Prophet's house; they made Iraq their centre and there the followers of error were combated by them – by al-Kufah with its science, jurists, grammarians, and famous men; by al-Basrah with its men of letters and

[38] Sa'id Pasha al-Mufti, then Prime Minister of Jordan.
[39] The Hashimites.

its grammarians. These were the servants of knowledge and the guardians of the Arabic language and of Islam.

In short, Iraq stands in the front rank. For while it is true that at times it has suffered from disturbances and uncertainties, it has shaken off these shortcomings and has become a refuge for the truth, a centre of sincerity, a homeland of our fathers, and a guide to the right way. One can judge the character of the land and people of Iraq from their steadfastness in the face of attempts to sway them from Sunnism to Shiism. Iraq at present includes the valleys of both the Tigris and the Euphrates and is protected from aggression by its remote position. For this reason Iraq, like Jordan, is able to speak the truth and disregard what certain persons say about it.

The Hashimite cause was propagated at al-Tafilah[40] and in greater Jordan by the Imam Muhammad ibn al-Hanafiyah[41] and by 'Ali ibn 'Abdallah ibn al-'Abbas. Abu Muslim al-Khurasani[42] received his instructions and directions from Jordan up to the time his movements became well established. This was the golden age of the Arabs. It is not to be wondered at, therefore, that even though other things may be forgotten the words of the poet will always remain:

> Should the horsemen of God one day
> be forbidden to ride forth
> My wish were that they should be freed
> by a Jordanian hand.

None of the descendants of al-Hasan and al-Husayn, of the Prophet's house, ever strove to set up a worldly empire; instead, whenever they saw a breach in the wall of Islam they issued a call for it to be repaired and for the structure to be raised higher. Since they served the true faith and protected it with their lives, each of these actions was a warning to those who worshipped the things of this world, lusted after wealth, and indulged in luxury and the things it brings in its train. Wrongdoers desisted from their excesses at the very thought of them, fearful of these attacks and war-cries which were like those of Muhammad and 'Ali. One should remember, therefore, that the differences of opinion which have been current

[40] A village in southern Jordan.

[41] A son of the Caliph 'Ali, in whose name Mukhtar raised his revolt in Iraq in 685–7. The part played by the Hashimite partisans in the fall of the Umayyad caliphate is well described by Bernard Lewis in his *The Arabs in History*, London, 1950, pp. 78–79.

[42] Leader of the Abbasid revolt in Iran beginning in 746.

since the Arab Revolt are an ancient malady and represent nothing new. Nevertheless, God watches over us.

Today it is Iraq and Jordan which bear the torch of unity and fear of God and which seek the truth, in the hope that those who are confused will rally to their banner and seek the shelter of true unity and Arabism. These two states do not suffer from the contentions of self-seekers, disseminators of seditious propaganda, and propagators of ambitions that do not lead to progress and security. This friction shows that those who wish to hold the Arabs back and prevent their progress are to be found elsewhere than in Iraq and Jordan.

Truth will prevail over all; falsehood may reign for a while, but it will fade away. May God give light to men's minds and illuminate the path for those who are hesitant and confused!

Egypt and the Arabs

I have already referred to Egypt and the fact that it is a member of the Arab League. But the Arabs and Egypt are two different things. The Arabs should be to Egypt as brother is to brother and Egypt should not ask the Arabs to halt the march of their progress because of Egypt's private problems. For he who wishes to gain all his rights in one day may find that he has lost them in the long run. We wish for Egypt what we wish for ourselves, and we believe that it behoves the Arabs to deal with the Egyptian question as they deal with their own problems. This should be on the basis to which I have already alluded – with due regard to our capabilities and the action that our sister countries which are concerned in the matter are able to take. Presented here for the reader is my frank letter on this subject to His Majesty King Faruq and his reply of 13 August 1947:

To His Majesty my brother King Faruq,
may God preserve him!

My dear Brother:
I pray for Your Majesty's prosperity and send my greetings and salutations. With Your Majesty's permission I send this letter of mine to your exalted throne in view of the heritage of friendship existing between our two houses, a friendship which I am eager to preserve because of my desire for the security of both our countries and houses.

It has been my hope that circumstances would permit us to meet and discuss the dangers facing us, as well as the disturbances to which we are exposed. But since the opportunity has not presented itself, the necessity of your grasping the nature of the situation as soon as possible has impelled me to speak as I am required to do by the duty of brotherhood, Arabism, and Islam.

There is no one on this earth who does not appreciate the patriotic blows struck by Egypt and the gradual progress it has made toward the desired goal in the reigns of your late father His Majesty King Fu'ad I and yourself. The present situation, indeed, causes one to tremble within oneself, to be anxious for the state of security, and to wish from the bottom of one's heart that the endeavours which have previously been made will be continued. I should like to point out that outworn customs, whether private or public, become a tyranny over men's minds and an arduous path on which it is difficult either to stop or turn back, since God in His strength has not sent us anyone who has sufficient personal qualities and patriotic feeling to free himself from the habits that impel our governments to travel a road which we ought to abandon for a better one.

There is no doubt but that at the beginning of your late father's reign it was the duty of the ruler and his aides to make manifest the desires of the people for liberation and independence. This plan has advanced steadily, but it is now felt that this drive should assume another form in order to gain the assistance of the entire Arab nation and its governments. Many opportunities to attain our goal have been lost through the quarrels and wranglings of our numerous political parties and various blocs. I praise God and trust that His Majesty my brother Faruq has the strength and firmness of judgement to lead his people himself, and through those of his people who are loyal to the throne and the nation direct them to the best and easiest way of employing their patriotism to attain that which is desired both by Egypt's monarch and its people. In the conduct of your noble ancestors from Muhammad 'Ali on you have a number of examples of how to deliver the nation from tyranny, excessive nationalism, and public disorder. His Majesty, then, if he pleases can decree what he considers necessary and can resolve to follow that path which he thinks preferable. The problems of Egypt are by their very nature shared by the rest of the Arab lands as well, for they are many bodies with but a single spirit.

The world situation, which has not brought peace to Europe, indicates that there are secular ideologies secretly at work which may cause war to flare up again. For the Russians on one hand and the Anglo-Saxons on the other are engaged in a fierce contest for supremacy, and small nations are impotent in the face of modern armaments and the staggering cost of war. It therefore becomes important that we look toward a firm understanding with the nations of the East, which would be followed by an alliance with the more familiar of the two camps within the framework of honour, independence, and unity of defence. For Iraq, Syria, and our beloved Egypt constitute the great core of the Middle East which could guarantee its safety from the covetousness of the greedy, if these three countries could only agree among themselves and find the right path.

In addition, we see that Greece, Turkey, and Iran are under the severest kind of pressure from the two camps. This is all the more reason for looking upon the Arab countries as united in spirit and for seeing that their numerous chiefs of state agree upon the drawing-up of a plan for the security of all. For joint defence imposes heavy burdens on us and makes it necessary for us to reconsider policy, which has been affected by the pressure of a newly-arisen public opinion both in Syria and in Egypt as well as here in Jordan.

Perhaps I might privately suggest to Your Majesty that if with God's help you were to order the resumption of the conversations between Egypt and Great Britain and postpone the submission of the question to the United Nations, Your Majesty might save Egypt and set its sister-nations at rest concerning their future, for they will certainly be involved in any new war. I am confident that the question of the unity of the Nile Valley will, with God's help, gradually be solved in accordance with the desires of Your Majesty. The world is guided by trust and divided by enmity, whether in word or in deed. This latter is a general misfortune which I hope Your Majesty will be able to overcome. I share your vigilance and solicitude and firmly believe that God is supporting you.

These things I speak sincerely before God because of my affection for Your Majesty. I kiss your eyes, my brother, and convey my highest regards for your person.

In the name of God the Merciful, the Compassionate.
From Faruq, by the grace of God,
King of Egypt and Lord of Nubia, the Sudan, Kordofan, and Darfur,
to His Majesty King 'Abdallah ibn al-Husayn,
King of the Hashimite Kingdom of Jordan.

My dear Brother:
I am grateful for my brother's honoured letter. May God grant success to his noble efforts and goodly aims and create between us mutual love in God, co-operation for the right, assistance for the good, and collaboration in action as a source of welfare and blessing, of strength and glory for us all.

I have been greatly touched by the concern shown in your letter for the various aspects of the situation in Egypt and for your eagerness that our affairs should develop in the most favourable fashion. I am conscious of the noble motives that have impelled you to write to me in one of the most critical periods through which my beloved country has passed. I am sure that the views which you have presented to me are most sincere and that you have imparted them because of your firm and steadfast love for me.

It is not surprising, therefore, that the clouds growing on the Egyptian horizon have affected your high-minded self in view of both the old and the new ties and the strong and noble bonds between us.

I most highly esteem the political views expressed in your letter regarding the benefit that would accrue to Egypt and all the Arab countries from a reopening of negotiations with Great Britain and the beneficial effects it could have in restoring trust as a guide for the world and in cleansing it of hostility in word and deed. I only wish that your letter had reached me at a time when I could have profited by your great experience, wide knowledge, and sound opinions. But my brother – may God strengthen him!–knows that God determines the fate of mankind and the end of all affairs. Every step that Egypt takes is directed by reliance on God and trust in a Lord who opens the door of hope only to him who seeks it.

My brother is deserving of my assurance that my government is making every effort possible to work for the realization of the goals which the people have set for themselves. It is concerned for and appreciates the delicate circumstances confronting small countries in a world agitated by momentous events.

It is a source of optimism for me that I can feel that Your Majesty shares Egypt's troubles and hopes and that Egypt's cause is the cause of all the Arabs. Every gain made by Egypt is a gain for these nations and peoples joined by an inseparable bond of language, religion, and unity of noble aims. This is an important factor making for faith and confidence.

My every hope is that God may make our future a good and blessed one and that my brother will accept my manifold thanks for the noble solicitude and honourable effort in which he is engaged.

I send Your Majesty the most sincere tokens of my love and my best greetings.

Faruq

Done at al-Qubbah Palace, 26 Ramadan 1366/13 August 1947 and in the tenth year of our reign.

So much for my views on Egypt and its policy with regard to the united Arab cause. It pains me to hear slanderous voices speaking from Egypt through its great newspapers, driving the Arab countries asunder and weakening the mainstay of their cohesion. They reveal clearly and plainly Egypt's attitude toward the Arabs and its desire to divest itself of its Arab character.

In this connection it might be appropriate to say a few words about the Egyptian press, for there are certain aspects of it which should be discussed for the good of Egypt and the Egyptians. Someone has coined a proverb which says, "Do not associate with a fool, for he will do you ill while wishing you well." The Egyptian press is interested in the welfare of its country, but in the case of certain of its representatives this takes second place to their own self-interest of pecuniary profit and expansion of circulation. These interests are commercial and serve to gain money for these papers while losing Egypt its friends. Here it is well to recall the words of the Arab poet:

> Wounds made by the lance are blamable,
> But there is no blame for those made by the tongue.

It is known, however, that neither the praise nor the slander dealt out by certain of these papers is of any consequence, for they hand out praise one day and insults the next as their motives shift. If they were to turn their attention to their own situation they would blush for shame; being what they are, however, they are not only unabashed by their own position but they even increase their washing of dirty linen in public.

Thus has a certain section of the Egyptian press alienated all of Egypt's best friends. As an example of this I may quote an article which appeared in the Cairo weekly *Akhir Sa'ah* of 21 June 1950 under the following heading:

WHO ARE WE?

Egypt of Today and Egypt of the Pharaohs

Five thousand years ago, on the banks of the Nile, the Egyptian race took its place in history and laid the first foundations of human civilization. Today, twenty million strong, we live on both banks of the Nile – but who are we? Are we the direct descendants of that stock which wrote the first pages of history? Or are we another people who entered this valley and were one of history's agents in changing everything in it? Are we a mixture of various races and without any single origin or stock?

The Spirit of Egypt

It may be that the answer to this question is not to be found in the clamorous streets of the cities; perhaps the remote countryside is the best field for investigation. Here are sombre villages of clusters of small, white-washed mud-brick dwellings grouped around the house of the *'umdah*.[43] Stores of grain

[43] The village headman.

and fuel are piled high on their roofs, and from them emanates the odour of bread mingled with the smell of domestic fowl and goats. Ranged above those stone mortars over there are rows of brick moulds which give off the reek of putrid earth. These are the same ancient Egyptian villages which have dotted the countryside for five thousand years and which are recorded in the papyri and on the walls of temples.

These fellahin still bend over the black earth and cultivate it regardless of the atomic explosions in the deserts of America and in the snows of Siberia. These unique figures, with their swarthy faces and remarkable quiet and uncomplaining spirit of self-immolation in the service of the soil from dawn to dark, have helped this hard-working people for whom even the building of the Pyramids was not too much. They have lived on this earth for five thousand years and they are the same peace-loving, gentle people who became valiant warriors under Rameses II and Thothmes III!

The Same Customs

Our present-day customs are the same as those of our forefathers fifty centuries ago. We learn from ancient papyri that life in Memphis the Beautiful was little different from life in Cairo a hundred years ago. The great gates flanking the city, guarded by watchmen night and day, lead to the main streets lined with shops and bustling with the activity of buying and selling. Fellahin come in from neighbouring villages to buy their necessities from the city's markets, but they do not depart until they have paid a visit to the temple of Ptah and presented offerings and gifts to its priests in quest for forgiveness and abundance. Despite the passage of time the same scenes are repeated today at the shrines of Sayyidah Zaynab and al-Husayn.[44]

Again, the Egyptian funeral procession which we see wending its way through the streets of Cairo to the cemetery is an exact replica of its ancient Egyptian counterpart in Thebes and Memphis. Religious rites described in the papyri record that the priests used to precede the coffin chanting sacred texts and burning incense. Then came the coffin, borne on the shoulders or resting on a cart drawn by animals, and followed first by the male mourners and then by the bare-bosomed women, their hair dishevelled and their countenances smeared with indigo and mud as they beat their faces, wail, and lament.

Separation from one's kinsfolk was the greatest ordeal the ancient Egyptian could experience, and the Egyptian family could not bear to be parted from one of its members. If by some hard fate the ancient Egyptian was forced to leave his country he fervently desired that he should die in Egypt and be buried in its sacred soil. Today, despite overpopulation and the need to emigrate as all other peoples do, we cling to life in Egypt and a feeling of being in exile afflicts every Egyptian whom fate has removed from his land.

The Truth as Science Sees It

Following this excursion, let us turn with our questions to those who make the truth their business – to the specialists in ancient Egyptian history. Let us go to the

[44] These two shrines are in Cairo.

44

neat villa on the Pyramid Road[45] which is the residence of Salim Bey Hasan, professor of Egyptian history. In his well-filled study we put these same questions to the learned professor. For a while he reflects upon them silently, then quietly smiles and replies: "Yes, we are Egyptians. There is no nation in the world which has preserved its original blood and stock as Egypt has. The Egyptian went to such extremes to guard his traditions, customs, and blood that in ancient times he used to marry his own sisters and daughters in order to keep his family strain pure and unmixed. The pharaohs in particular paid close attention to the preservation of the purity of the royal blood. The pharaoh would never permit a daughter of his to marry another king, in order that the divine royal Egyptian blood should not be mixed with that of the foreigner.[46]

"Others claim that the Egyptian stock has been diluted with non-Egyptian stock such as the Greek, the Arab, the Asiatic, and others. This has led some people to the inaccurate belief that the people of Egypt are a mixture of these stocks and that the proportion of Egyptian blood remaining is small – a claim that is totally erroneous. The fact is that Egypt has preserved its blood and stock up to the present in spite of the invasion of its territories by these other ethnic groups. The present Egyptian people, therefore, are the descendants of their ancient Egyptian forebears.

"The conquerors of Egypt penetrated only into the large cities such as Memphis, Thebes, and Alexandria; the countryside and Upper Egypt were preserved from admixture with these conquerors. We find, for example, that when Alexander the Great conquered Egypt the Greeks built a special settlement for themselves and that they have lived down to the present without mixing with the Egyptians. Then, too, when they invaded Egypt they did not exceed four thousand in number; they did not intermarry with the Egyptians, and abstain from doing so to this day. The nomadic Bedouin who wander about the Egyptian countryside likewise refuse adamantly to intermarry with the fellahin. Therefore, we find that the Egyptian who inhabited the rural areas of Egypt five thousand years ago is the same as the Egyptian of today.

"Investigation has indicated that ancient Egyptian skulls recently discovered in excavations in various parts of the country are no different from the skulls of modern Egyptians. This provides concrete evidence which does not admit of doubt.

"In religious traditions also you find that the Egyptian has coloured his Islamic faith with the religion and customs of ancient Egypt. For this reason we find that the legends and folk-tales of ancient Egypt still survive in Muslim Egypt, a phenomenon that can be found in no other Muslim country."

[45] In the Cairo suburb of Giza.

[46] While this was true in the pre-Empire period, it was not true particularly after the reign of Thutmose IV. See John A. Wilson, *The Burden of Egypt*, Chicago, 1951, pp. 201–202.

45

Another Truth

Among the ruins of Luxor, Professor Mekhitarian,[47] director of the Queen Elizabeth Foundation in Brussels for the study of Egyptian antiquities, considers the question, then removes his hat and replies:

"The people of present-day Egypt are a direct survival of the ancient Egyptian stock. In spite of the many invasions of Egypt by neighbouring peoples, these conquerors – like all others – lived in the large cities away from the Egyptian population until there arose an Egyptian leader who drove them completely out and occupied the throne of Egypt. All you have to do is to look at the people's faces and their manner of living, and you will realize the truth of what I say.

"All that happened when the Arabs entered Egypt was that the majority of the Egyptians embraced the Muslim faith as they had previously accepted Christianity, while only a minority have remained Copts down to the present. This does not mean in any sense that the Egyptians became Arabs. If you want a precise figure, I should say that not less than 85 per cent of the present-day people of Egypt are descendants of the ancient Egyptians."

I am patient with nationalist ignorance, however, and persevere in my efforts to win for the Arab peoples a position of pre-eminence and honour, whether the lands they live in are nearby or far away. I do not conceal my joy at Libya's attaining the first stage of its independence or at the decisions France has taken regarding Tunisia. I fervently hope that we shall see the Hashimite State of Morocco attain its complete and genuine independence through an honourable understanding with France and Spain. I reproduce here a message which I sent to the valiant leader 'Abd al-Karim al-Khattabi on 4 Dhu al-Hijjah 1368 (26 September 1949):

Your Highness:

You know, my brother, that I keep nothing from men like yourself, our outstanding protagonist, however confidential it might be. I should like to point out that the Arab League's failure in the Palestine question has been a great dishonour to the Arabs and that they must arouse themselves to regain their glory and honour. It is not merely through expressions of sympathy that this can be achieved, but through intelligence, wisdom, and deliberation.

God warned us against disunity, but we did not pay heed. It is with the greatest sorrow that I say that I feel that those among us who are leading us astray are still being hearkened to; but we must not lose faith in the spirit of God, for only unbelievers could do that. Nor should we give up the hope

---

[47] A. Mekhitarian is an assistant in the Ancient Egyptian Section of the Queen Elizabeth Foundation in Brussels.

that your beloved country will reach a cultural and economic level even higher than that which you are seeking. I have often spoken of you and your country, though I have not found much sympathy for my words. But put your trust in God and His good intentions; write to your friends and advise them to provide the cultural and economic co-operation which you have requested. On my part, God willing, I shall endeavour to guarantee everything else.

Anglo-Arab Relations

The Arab East cannot be strong unless it is unified and secure and unless it stands together so as to be able to ensure all its rights and protect its honour and dignity.

First of all, it must be unified. The first step in this direction is the unification of historical Syria, to be followed by its union with Iraq and by an endeavour to raise the level of education in the Hijaz, Najd, and the Yemen to the plane of that prevailing under modern governments. The character of the Arabs and of the Muslim religion is sufficiently broad to accommodate itself to the needs of the present day and the requirements of modern states in the fields of economics, industry, and national defence. It is the duty of Great Britain to comprehend this and reach an understanding with the Arab League states in these matters after the bonds which have confined the Arab will in the Arab states have been loosened and an opportunity has been provided for the expression of suppressed desires and the exercise of rights that have been restricted and limited.

Great Britain, indeed, is broad-minded and progressive in its agreements, as has been remarked by the realists both in the case of the Bevin-Sidqi agreement[48] and the Bevin-Salih Jabr agreement.[49] As the owner of al-Ghabra' said to the horse Dahis,[50] "Little by little they run the course." The course is the same for all; not every starter is doomed to defeat, but neither is he guaranteed victory in the race. It is up to every people to know its own capabilities and to finish its course in the allotted time. The years of preparation in Germany between World Wars I and II were not easy

[48] On the solution of the Suez question; October 1946.

[49] The Anglo-Iraqi so-called "Portsmouth Treaty" of 16 January 1948.

[50] This refers to an Arab horse race which took place in the 6th century and was the cause of inter-tribal strife for long afterward. See P. K. Hitti, *History of the Arabs*, 5th ed., New York, 1951, p. 90.

ones for the German people, nor was the accomplishment of the Five-Year Plan easy for Soviet Russia. Particularly in these modern times progress makes demands on the abilities of states in the building of roads and airfields, the training of airmen, the building-up of reserves of material, and the construction of arms factories so that in time of war there will be no lack of weapons.

The Jewish–Arab problem is witness to the truth of what I say, and it is the duty of those friendly countries which are involved in the question to show their affection for this part of the East and develop a sincere friendship with it. They should not deprive it of necessities in time of need; they should come to an understanding with the Arab East and win the support of this area as a whole. On the other hand, the Arabs should understand that the past two World Wars have abolished the rule of one nation over another. The nations of the world have awakened and are on their guard; their peoples are no longer willing to tolerate the presence of the forces of states desiring to extend their control over such small nations as might strike their fancy. The leaders of the Arabs can accept what I have said with the fullest confidence and faith in my good intentions toward our people.

Chapter 2
Travels and Missions

My Visit to London;
the Modification of the Original Anglo-Jordanian Treaty;
the Amir Is Designated King

I have been following the slow course of our gradual progress and the expansion of our national rights. I have given due consideration to every aspect of the question as it touches various countries, including both our neighbouring sister Arab states and the mandatory state.[1]

My visit to Great Britain was in response to an invitation issued by the present Labour government in 1946.[2] At that time the Prime Minister of Transjordan was His Excellency Ibrahim Hashim Pasha. The visit began auspiciously, since both the Labour government and Mr Bevin were then enjoying a high degree of popularity. The Bevin–Ibrahim Hashim treaty was concluded, as a result of which Transjordan was elevated from an amirate to a kingdom;[3] it became known as The Hashimite Kingdom of the Jordan[4] and its complete sovereignty and independence were recognized.

The Inshas[5] Conference

Following my visit to London I was invited by H.M. King Faruq to attend the conference at Inshas. The invitation to this conference had been accepted by the heads of all the Arab states with the exception of the Imam Yahya of the Yemen and the Saudis, who were content with sending H.R.H. Prince 'Abdallah and H.R.H. Crown Prince Sa'ud respectively. It was a valuable opportunity for the heads of these states to meet on an important matter. H.M. King Faruq displayed the greatest kindness and affection toward his

[1] Great Britain.

[2] This visit took place in February–March 1946.

[3] This treaty was signed in Amman on 15 March 1948.

[4] The Jordanian Official Gazette on 1 June 1949 announced that from December 1948 the name of the country had been changed to The Hashimite Kingdom of the Jordan.

[5] An estate of ex-King Faruq near Ismailia. The conference took place on 25 May 1946.

honoured guests and made plain his good intentions and his resolution to make every sacrifice in the cause for which these heads of state had been assembled.

That which transpired at this conference is well established and well known, but the backsliding which soon took place among the Arabs was not Egypt's fault. It was due to a certain individual who arrived in Egypt and began to work to the detriment of the Arabs and Palestine; this person was al-Hajj Amin al-Husayni, known as the Mufti. Incidentally, I was aware that he had received from Shukri al-Quwwatli, President of Syria, a large sum of money amounting to 250,000 Syrian pounds, which was only a small part of what he received from other sources. Thus was our unity of purpose disrupted.

After the outbreak of the fighting in Palestine I made a visit to Egypt between the first and the second cease-fires[6] to inform myself personally of the views of H.M. King Faruq in Cairo and of those of his government. In addition, I wished to investigate the case of the material belonging to the Arab Legion which had been confiscated by Egypt at the beginning of hostilities and to obtain permission to visit the Egyptian forces at the front. I received fair promises, but for reasons unknown to me I was unable to accomplish anything. It is not my place, however, to go into this matter further. This was followed by the events which have been described at the beginning of these memoirs.[7]

My Visit to Najd[8]

On this occasion I met with H.M. King Ibn Sa'ud and acquainted myself with his opinions and his good faith. Our views were sent to the Arab League, which at the time was meeting in Cairo. Upon returning to Baghdad I was surprised to hear from H.E. Muzahim al-Pachachi[9] of the breaking of the cease-fire in Palestine, which resulted in the irretrievable loss of Lydda and al-Ramlah. In spite of the fact that I bore the title of Commander in Chief, both Egypt and Iraq made various excuses for not having sought my advice during the fighting.

I must say a word concerning the personality of King 'Abd al-Aziz ibn Sa'ud as I discovered it to be during my visit to him. His Majesty, I agree, is one of the political geniuses of the Arabs in this

[6] This visit took place in June 1948.
[7] See above, p. 22.
[8] See above, p. 23, and n. 37, ch.I.
[9] Then Prime Minister of Iraq.

day and age. He is a pleasant companion, and though gruff in speaking is gentle and graceful in speech and is extremely hospitable – may God grant him sons and grandsons and whatever favours it is His pleasure to bestow! During his career he had come to grips with two Arab chieftains of tremendous courage, but he knew how to overcome and destroy them. I now entertain a heartfelt respect for His Majesty, since he acceded to my wish for a frank discussion of political matters, did not avoid realities, and was straightforward in setting forth his plans. Of all the family, Prince Sa'ud enjoys in my estimation a place second only to that of his father.

Najd of today is not the same country that I once knew; it is now traversed by automobiles and aeroplanes that have taken the place of the camel which had been its means of transportation since ancient times. Al-Zahran (Dhahran) has its oil wells, and I saw a new road which was being built to connect the villages of southern Najd with the coast. There was no opportunity for me to visit and inspect the Hijaz. I have heard, however, that the Hijazi youth who have returned from college are well-equipped with knowledge and education. To all the inhabitants of the Hijaz, who from of old have been known for their intelligence and aptitude, I wish success for the future.

My Visit to Turkey:
Presidents Ismet Inönü and Calal Bayar

I still remember my visit to the new Turkey in 1947 at the invitation of its respected President Ismet Inönü. If this invitation was indicative of anything, it was that our brethren in the East considered that the rejuvenation of our glory lay in true mutual understanding and fraternal support of each other. This is what we should have done long ago when Europe began to awaken and when the Austrian Empire began to attack the European possessions of the Ottoman state. Czarist Russia was moving against the Ukraine, the Crimea, and the area around the sea of Azov in the Caucasus. That was the time when the people of the East, both Turks and Arabs, should have rejuvenated themselves by forming strong local cadres linked with the centre of the empire. If this had taken place the Muslim countries would have been spared the evils which befell them and the weakness which afflicted the centre of the empire without benefiting its periphery. It is my hope that from now on we shall see these things come to pass and, if God so wills, form federations from Pakistan in the southeast to Edirne in the northwest and from the borders of Tibet in the east to Tangier in the west.

I departed from Haifa on the President's private yacht *Savarona*, which is well known for the beauty of its design, the elegance of its furnishings, the excellence of its discipline, and for its ability to sport with the waves as the waves play with it. It brought us to the harbour of Alexandretta in sixteen hours, and after it had anchored we went ashore. The reception committee was headed by our Minister to Turkey Badri Bey Shaman, the learned son of a learned father. There we boarded the President's private train and travelled with the Taurus Mountains before us, passing through one valley after another. The land began to grow more beautiful and was adorned with various kinds of flowers and trees. We ascended hills and descended through valleys, through which streams flowed while rain descended, accompanied sometimes by hail and snow, obscurity and clouds, so that we had a fitful view of the scenery until night finally closed in while we were still in the midst of the mountains.

The train itself was everything one could desire – a well-appointed palace or a travelling castle, if you wish. It contained all kinds of modern and luxurious features, splendid appointments and furnishings in its compartments and sleeping and eating quarters. All this was a pleasure and a delight, for life in this world is but the enjoyment of vanities – moments of joy and gladness followed by years of evil caused by wickedness which provides merriment to the malevolent and revulsion to the good.

By way of this chain of mountains and valley slopes we had been approaching the plains of Anatolia. I shall never forget the meanderings of the Jeyhan[10] River, which the traveller to Ankara keeps on his left, stretched out like a winding, sinuous, silver thread and bringing abundance and water to the land. Since its channel and dams are maintained and its flow is regulated, it waters the land without damaging it, all of this being accomplished by gravity. As a consequence the fellah is happy with his present lot and has hope for the future.

We continued travelling through the countryside, which, though tenanted in the past, had not yet been completely restored to production; here and there one could see both cultivated and uncultivated land. On 8 January 1947 we reached Ankara and found the station filled with a large crowd at the head of which was

[10] The text has Jayhun, which is the name for the Oxus in Central Asia; this is a slip for the very similar Jeyhan, the classical Pyramus in Cilicia.

President Ismet Inönü. Although he is already well known to my readers, I should like to say a few words about him.

Ismet Inönü is an outstanding military leader. In the first part of my memoirs I mentioned that he had been chief of staff of General Izzet Pasha, who had been sent to restore the situation in the Yemen in the time of Sultan Mehmet V[11] and who conferred with my late father[12] concerning the Yemen while passing through Jidda. He became acquainted with Palestine in World War I; at the battle of Inönü, from which he took his name, he performed deeds to which the human tongue cannot do justice. The missions he undertook during the San Remo peace conference[13] and the negotiations among Iraq, Turkey, and England on the Mosul question[14] are well known and famous. It is unnecessary to expatiate on his long tenure of the premiership of Turkey in the time of Atatürk.

Upon my leaving the train His Excellency approached to shake my hand and embrace me, after which I inspected the troops which were drawn up in welcome. Following this I was driven to the well-known Ankara Palace Hotel, where I was to stay. With me was Muhammad al-Shurayqi Pasha, then my Foreign Minister and at present Minister of Palace Affairs.

After spending five days in Istanbul, where I was lodged at Dolma Bahçe Palace, I returned by train directly to Alexandretta and thence by presidential yacht to Haifa, pleased and extremely grateful. Our security today is encompassed by brotherhood between the nations of the East, a fraternal relationship that cannot be marred by elements of doubt or suspicion.

The long-continued premiership of Inönü has represented years of recuperation for Turkey; it has been a period of trial during which he has learned who the sincere and who the insincere friends of Turkey were. He left the premiership as a result of the recent elections[15] in which the Turkish Democratic Party, headed by Calal Bayar, was victorious. Both men had served as Prime Minister in the days of Atatürk and were experienced in that office. Ismet Inönü is a rare soldier, a distinguished statesman, and a true Turk, but this world always grows tired of its sons. When President Bayar looks about him he can see that he has a wide field for action, both in initiating works of his own and in completing what has been left

[11] This was in 1910–1911.
[12] Sharif Husayn.
[13] 1920.
[14] 1925–1926.
[15] 14 May 1950.

undone. He can create the most valuable opportunities for those who are interested in the general welfare of Turkey, and his works will be received with gratitude and esteem.

During this visit we concluded a treaty of friendship and amity between my kingdom and the Republic of Turkey,[16] in regard to which our statesmen issued the following joint communiqué:

On the occasion of the visit of His Majesty 'Abdallah ibn al-Husayn, King of the Hashimite Kingdom of Jordan, to the Republic of Turkey, close contacts have been made between the statesmen of the two countries and friendly and comprehensive discussions have been carried on regarding the peace of the Near and Middle East and relations between the two states.

As a result of these discussions it has become evident to each of these two states that they both have the same ideals of peace and international solidarity. These ideals constitute the aims of the national policy of both states, which is inspired by a unity of interest, mutual friendship, and the concept of co-operation with all neighbouring countries. These common feelings have resulted in the signing of a treaty of friendship to the benefit of both countries.

My Visit to Iran: Brotherhood in Islam

I had been paid an unexpected visit by the Iranian Minister in Beirut, Zayn al-'Abidin Rahnoma, recently-appointed Iranian Minister in Amman. He conveyed to me His Majesty the Shah of Iran's wish that I be invited to visit His Majesty at some suitable time. Since this proposal coincided with an already existing desire on my part, I told the Minister that such a visit would create friendship and fraternal feeling and would be a great honour to me. He replied, "In that case here is the invitation, which I have with me." I promised to make the visit, which he urged should be as soon as possible after the end of Ramadan AH 1368[17]; and so, praise be to God, it came to pass.

My route led via Baghdad, where I was pleased to see H.R.H. my brother the Amir Zayd and other Iraqis. After spending a night with them I continued by air to Tehran. I pondered over the history of the past and the bonds of tradition and affiliation that bound Iran to the Hashimite house. As we left the Arab plains of Iraq and began to enter Iran's highlands and mountains with their snow-covered

---

[16] Signed at Ankara on 11 January 1947.
[17] After 26 July 1948.

peaks and networks of valleys, towns, and villages, there came to my mind the history of the pre-Islamic kings of Iran and its greatness and rise to power under Islam. I thought of its learned men, who rendered service to the Arabic language and who included some of the greatest names in every field of activity. From the air we could see Isfahan, then Mount Damavand; the closer we approached to Tehran the greater became my desire to meet the gracious ruler and his land and people.

When one's memory fails one becomes dull. It is easy for a writer or speaker to describe nature – the earth with its plains and mountains, the sea in its calm and its boisterous moods, the steady pouring of the rain, the violence and flashing of the lightning, the buoyancy of good health, and the fatigue of illness. But not every writer or speaker can accurately describe the feelings he experiences and his preoccupation with what he wishes to say to a person whom he does not know and when he meets one whom he loves.

The weather was clear, but we kept going up and down because of air pockets until we jokingly said that we had become thoroughly familiar with the atmosphere of the land of Shiism, which perhaps was trying to test our courage. As we arrived over the outskirts of Tehran we were met by Iranian aeroplanes flying in groups of four; these manoeuvred around us in welcome and then made off so that the special aeroplane which was carrying us could land. Upon our touching the ground I uttered the words, "Our course and its end are in the name of God; my Lord is indeed forgiving and merciful!"

At the airport we found a reception committee which preceded us to where lines of people were waiting to welcome us. There we met His Majesty, surrounded by his ministers, various notables of the country, the royal family, and the ambassadors of friendly foreign countries. As he greeted me he clasped my hand with a smile and we embraced as father and son, or as brothers, if you will. Then he introduced me to the various men, princes, leaders, and ambassadors, whom he wished me to meet and in return I presented my suite to him.

After inspecting the guard of honour we entered one of the royal automobiles. The Shah began welcoming me in Persian and astonished me by saying, "I am the simplest of the servants of Islam and the Muslims and you are descended from an ancient line of rulers. Your visit gives great pride and is a mark of respect and honour. If Your Majesty should so desire, I am prepared to bring all the Muslims together and create true brotherhood among the nations of Islam. Whatever one undertakes with good will and with a desire to please God is certain of success. This I am ready to do." I replied as best I could, praising him for his aims and thanking him for the objective which he had expressed. "The matter which Your Majesty has raised," I answered, "is in your hands; it is what I desire and I give it my support."

As we were exchanging expressions of our feelings of Islamic brotherhood I had been noticing the people lining both sides of the street to greet their ruler and his guest with their well-known courtesy, graciousness, and hospitality. At length we reached Saheb-e Garaniyeh Palace, which had been prepared for my residence. His Majesty took my hand as we ascended the stairs and reached the great hall of Iran, glittering with crystal on its ceiling and walls. Following the reception His Majesty received from me the exalted Order of the Renaissance with diamonds and the collar of al-Husayn ibn 'Ali, the highest decorations I could present to a person such as His Majesty. In return he bestowed upon me the Order of Pahlavi, first class, and the Royal Collar. His Majesty then left the palace with expressions of esteem and honour and with an invitation to visit him at Sa'dabad Palace in half an hour.

During my visit to the Shah at Sa'dabad Palace we concluded our discussions regarding the formation of an Islamic front. My days in Iran were taken up with functions and visits. I was pleased with what I saw and was impressed by the military activity and efficiency of the high army leaders and officers, which clearly indicated that there was no weakness of morale or lax leadership. The good impressions I gained from my visit to Iran were made public by me at a press conference held for me in Tehran, on which occasion I gave the following message to the magnanimous Iranian people:

To the noble people of Iran:

I was greatly pleased at the invitation of my dear brother the Shahinshah of Iran to visit him and my beautiful sister country. Since the arrival of my companions and myself we have experienced the affection that has radiated from the skies of Iran, the magnitude of its graciousness, its brotherly welcome, and the attachment of its most noble people. I treasure this as the most beautiful of my memories. The special place which we of the Prophet's house have in our hearts for the people of Iran, and the memorials and eternal spiritual connections which we have in Iran make our love for our sister Muslim country a most natural one.

I have, in truth, been most impressed by the works of the departed great leader of Iran, the late Reza Shah Pahlavi, and by the way in which His Majesty his gracious son has followed in his footsteps and continued his work. This work represents a beneficent line of action which has brought forth great reforms and noticeable progress in a short time and in a period fraught with difficulties. This will bring about the dawn of a brilliant future and is the harbinger of well-being for a noble people. The mainstay of the future lies in the sincere devotion of the people to His Majesty their beloved ruler and in the tangible zeal of His Majesty on behalf of his loyal people, aided by the strength of God and the blessings of His chosen Prophet; may God bless him and grant peace to him and to his family.

As an official result of the contacts between His Majesty the Shah and myself the statesmen of our two countries issued the following joint statement:[18]

On the occasion of the visit to Iran of His Majesty the King of the Hashimite Kingdom of the Jordan, the representatives of the two states, being desirous of strengthening the friendly ties prevailing between these two states, have taken the opportunity to exchange views on the subject of co-operation as it affects the interests of both states, whether in commercial or cultural matters or in political relations.

The two parties therefore have agreed to the following:

1. The strengthening of friendly relations between the two countries by the conclusion of a treaty of friendship between them.[19]

2. The creation of economic ties between the two states through the conclusion of a treaty of commerce.

3. The creation of educational and cultural co-operation between the two countries.

4. Political co-operation in the international field on behalf of world peace and the stabilization of security and freedom, with due regard to the charter of the United Nations Organization and without prejudice to the obligations of the Hashimite Kingdom of the Jordan under the charter of the League of Arab States.

5. The making of joint efforts to resolve by peaceful means disputes which may arise between Muslim states; an endeavour to bring about good understanding and co-operation among them; and the strengthening of their economic and cultural ties. This shall not prevent either of the two states from accepting any proposal agreed to by the Muslim states for better ordering and co-ordinating relations among themselves.

My Visit to Britain

When I returned from Tehran I had hoped that the Shah might

[18] This statement was issued on 7 August 1949.

[19] Such a treaty was signed on 16 November 1949.

visit me in Amman at the earliest opportunity. But I had been in my capital hardly two days when I departed for Great Britain.[20] En route I had wanted to meet with His Majesty the King of Egypt to remove certain misconceptions which may have entered his mind concerning the events that had taken place at Beersheba, as a result of which the Egyptian forces retreated from Hebron and Bethlehem and rejoined their main force on the coast.

I did not succeed in meeting His Majesty owing to the fact that he was vacationing on the Mediterranean, but I had an audience with His Excellency Husayn Sirri Pasha, then Prime Minister, and with 'Azzam Pasha, who is Secretary General of the Arab League and an old friend known to all. Sirri Pasha fully understood the explanations I presented to him. Because of the favourable impression this meeting made on me owing to the Prime Minister's reasonableness and his love of the East, I was moved after my return to prompt my then Minister of Palace Affairs, H. E. Samir Pasha a-Rifa'i, to dispatch to His Excellency the following letter manifesting my desire to clear the atmosphere between the King of Egypt and myself and expressing the hopes I entertained for the welfare of beloved Egypt and its noble people:

His Excellency Husayn Sirri Pasha,
Chief of the Royal Cabinet

My dear Excellency:

I present to Your Excellency my best greetings and greatest respect. I have the honour to inform Your Excellency that in accordance with the royal wishes of His Majesty my sovereign I am directing this personal message to Your Excellency to state that in the interview with Your Excellency which took place in Alexandria, and which I had the honour to attend as a member of His Majesty's suite, Your Excellency showed the most complete understanding of the wishes for well-being and happiness and the attainment of our sister Egypt's hopes and aspirations which His Hashimite Majesty entertains toward His Majesty the great ruler of Egypt and toward Egypt and its noble people. Your Excellency will recall likewise that his Majesty had desired to make a side trip to Egypt during his return from Spain last summer, but was prevented from doing so by circumstances and by certain influences known to Your Excellency.

I do not doubt that Your Excellency, like me, believes that time is passing quickly and that the harm to which the interests of our countries are exposed, because of certain already-existing political orientations,

[20] This visit took place between 18 August and 3 September 1949.

make it imperative for us all to take serious action to remove the influences which have provoked this attention and that we must make every possible effort to promote friendly relations and increase the fraternal ties between our two kingdoms and peoples, particularly the noble royal houses and the two great rulers. If Your Excellency should be so good as to give due consideration and encouragement to this view of mine and find that the present time is suitable for the taking of effective steps to this noble end, I on my part am entirely prepared to carry out my part in any common effort which Your Excellency might think it advisable to take for this high purpose.

In anticipation of the favourable judgement which Your Excellency may be pleased to express on this subject, I trust that Your Excellency will accept my assurances of respect and esteem. Peace be upon you.

Yours sincerely,
Samir al-Rifa'i, Minister of the Hashimite Court

19 February 1950

His Excellency Samir al-Rifa'i Pasha,
Minister of the Hashimite Court

My dear Excellency:
It is with thanks and esteem that I have received your letter revealing the gracious desire of His Majesty King 'Abdallah.

Your Excellency knows more than anyone that Egypt has always made the greatest possible effort to strengthen the bonds of affection and friendship between the Arab peoples and that it has never deviated from this line, as I assured Your Excellency during our meeting in Alexandria.

I share Your Excellency's feelings of deep regret at the political orientations which have had their repercussions on the beloved hopes and noble aims which it had been expected that the Arab League would realize.

It gives me pleasure to tell my gracious brother that the high feelings expressed by His Hashimite Majesty are esteemed by His Majesty who occupies the throne of Egypt. I pray to God that He may fortify us with His strength, guide us with His wisdom, keep well-being and blessings in store for us, and grant us success in that which is in the interest of our countries. I trust that you will convey to His Majesty my deepest expressions of thanks for the distinguished effort and illustrious objective which he has revealed.

Peace and the mercy of God be upon you.
Husayn Sirri, Chief of His Majesty's Cabinet

27 February 1950

Following my side trip to Egypt I continued on to England, where I found the greatest support for the idea of an Islamic front. This attitude was demanded by the interests of Great Britain, who would be the friend of Islam everywhere if she could only find those who would understand her and profit by British advice, experience, and strength. More important, when I visited their Majesties King George VI and the Queen at Balmoral Castle in Scotland I found a warm welcome, family affection, much sincere friendship, and firm trust. I spoke, of course, with His Majesty and found that he was fully informed of and genuinely pleased with the prevailing good understanding, both personal and official, between myself and His Majesty's Government. Afterwards, the American Ambassador in London met with me and I spoke to him of what Iran's needs were in the way of quick facilities for development. The Ambassador became interested in this and his return to his country was followed by the Shah's visit to Washington.[21] What happened there and its sequel are the concern of His Majesty and the American Government; I know nothing beyond certain indications that there were good results.

My Visit to Spain[22];
Hopes for the Realization of the Aspirations
of the Arabs of Morocco

Upon my return from Great Britain I received an invitation from General Franco, the Spanish Chief of State. There were things about His Excellency and his people which had aroused my admiration and esteem and brought forth my affection. He is one of my greatest personal friends and I trust that in the near future there will come about good understanding between the great democracies and Spain.

The world should understand the similarity of character and manner of government that exists between the Arabs and Spain, for it seems to me that patriarchal rule by a single hand is preferable to other types of government. I hope that we shall see General Franco take firm and correct steps to realize the hopes of the Moroccan Arabs, between whom and the General there are well-known connections, in order that he and caliphal Morocco may reach friendship and agreement of a kind which will not wound the hearts of the Arabs wherever they may be.

[21] The Shah arrived in Washington on 16 November 1949.
[22] King 'Abdallah arrived in Spain on 5 September 1949 and left for Beirut on 18 September.

On my return I travelled aboard a Spanish warship as far as Lebanon. There is no need to repeat what happened during the few hours I spent as a guest of His Excellency Shaykh Bisharah al-Khuri,[23] except to say that I was pleasantly received and entertained. I noticed, however, that for some unknown reason precautions were taken to prevent persons who wished to meet me from doing so.

[23] Then President of Lebanon.

Chapter 3
International Problems

Communism, Democracy, and Other Ideologies

The British readers of my memoirs have desired to know my opinions on world affairs. This by its very nature is a delicate task for me, for they have much broader experience than I and are better able to assess world events and trends. Nevertheless, I shall try.

European civilization and the imperialism of the Western powers have found a fertile field in the countries of Islam and in North, West, and South Africa. The last accomplishment of this offspring of European civilization was the destruction of the Abyssinian empire, despite the fact that it was Christian. For a long time Russia had been dealing blow after blow to the Ottoman Empire. This aroused the feelings and sensitivity of the East. The stirring of Asia began with the awakening of Japan, followed by that of China as a result of the ten-year Sino–Japanese war.[1] The people of China, feeling that they should be true Chinese, refused to follow Chiang Kai-shek, whom they believed to be acting on behalf of others. Because of the proximity of Russia's frontiers to China, Stalin's propaganda had a profound effect on those who were desirous of attaining power in China with foreign help, as Chiang Kai-shek had accepted aid from America and the democracies. Then came communism.

Communism is a transient creed, a blinding flash which dazzles men's eyes until its true nature and the evil and immorality that lie behind it become known and are rejected. There is an awakening in China and there is strength there. The yellow race, extending from Tibet to Bukhara and as far as the Urals, is one stock and one colour: it is the colour of Asia.

Two great wars have ruined and exhausted Europe. Germany does not exist and the Austrian Empire is forgotten. France's colonies are quaking under her feet, while France itself has been

[1] This seems to refer to the conflict between China and Japan in the years 1933–1941.

crushed by the war. Italy has failed in its objectives, and there is no security from the Yellow Peril and communism except in Islam and the lands where it prevails.

Islam is a stable creed with a rich history and a strong courage united under the slogans of: "There is no god but God, and Muhammad is the Apostle of God"; "There is no rule except God's"; "Tyrants are the enemies of God"; and "Justice is the basis of dominion". Only good faith on the part of both the nations of Western Europe and the Muslim East can prevent the latter from standing by itself as a barrier between East and West. The Muslim East, however, must be genuinely Muslim and not corrupted in morals, imitating others in its way of life, or hesitant in its faith. Otherwise I believe that we shall see a succession of uprisings under various guises and names. It would mean a quick and terrible end to the civilized world in spite of those who are serving the cause of peace and who love humanity.

I have heard of a strange idea attributed to Mr Churchill, Britain's leader in the recent World War: the unification of the armies of Europe to meet the communist Russian threat. In this case one wonders why this leader put a complete end to Germany in the recent war without giving thought to Russia, which has assumed the place of Germany. How can the nations of Europe unify their armies and thereby still maintain their racial and national character? If this signifies anything, it is that each faction is desirous of obtaining for itself the lion's share of the world's goods.

Even stranger than all this is the fact that while the democracies are on hostile terms with communism, they nevertheless maintain ambassadors in Moscow while the Communists have ambassadors in Washington and London. Yet there is no ambassador from America or England in Madrid, which is the enemy of communism. The peoples of the world have recognized that despotism is the foundation upon which the destructive doctrines of communism, Nazism, and fascism are built and that their aim is to oppress small nations. If Nazism grew up and became strong in Germany it was because the German people were prepared to accept such principles and were willing to plunge into war. Since they were unable to dominate the situation they grew increasingly tyrannical and were destroyed, as was the case with fascism as well.

If communism had not found a field of play in Asia it would have turned its attention to the West and would have endeavoured to expand in Europe. But the various nations of Western Europe are not of the kind to acquiesce in the loss of their historical tradition or resign themselves to an autocratic rule that would exile, tyrannize over, and oppress them as it wished. Therefore, the difficulties which communism faces in Europe are similar to those which block its path in the lands of Islam. The protagonists of this tyrannical doctrine would be well advised to call a halt where they stand at present, for if Hitler had stopped only one day before the recent war broke out he would still be alive. History is full of such cases.

My advice to the democracies is to seek a fraternal relation with the peoples of Islam, whom they know and with whom they have been on friendly terms; they should trust them, help them attain their aims, and give complete recognition to their rights. In this way a balance of world forces would be attained and mankind would be freed from the evils of war and propaganda. If such an understanding could be reached, everyone being satisfied with what he possesses and recognizing his responsibilities, there would be no fertile field for intrigue, and as long as the Muslim peoples possessed the means to defend their homelands they would not be afraid to do so.

The effective remedy for the problem of the defence of Western Europe in the event of Soviet aggression lies in three things: a serious reconsideration of the matter of putting an end to the anomalous situation in Central Europe; the restoration of the German army by creating a fraternal feeling between Germany and western nations such as France and Belgium; and removal of the causes of vindictiveness and hostility between them.

The Muslim World

I cannot, of course, neglect to discuss the Muslims and the responsibilities they bear in the era of world revolutions and surprises. As they exist at present, the territories of Islam extend continuously in a unit from Tibet to Gibraltar, from Edirne to Pakistan, and from the shores of the Black Sea to the Pacific Ocean. They constitute a single bloc with one faith, and the individual countries and peoples can survive, grow, and become strong only if they all hold fast to that in which they believe; they must defend their homelands with the courage, sincerity, and purity of faith for which these peoples are well known. The Muslims form a compact structure, each part of which supports the other. It was for this reason that God imposed upon them the duty of the annual pilgrimage so that they might meet at the hub of Islam and return home benefited, firmer in brotherhood, and stronger in their attachment to God and country. It is their duty to put their own national and historic sciences and their religion on a par with the preferential position of the modern sciences in their educational systems.

As I have said, the pilgrimage is both a religious duty and a means of establishing mutual acquaintance and brotherly feeling. God (may He be praised and exalted!) has said, "And when we established for Abraham the place of the house of God we said, 'Do not associate any other god with Me, but cleanse My house for those who circumambulate it and for those who pray standing, bowing, or prostrating themselves. And proclaim the pilgrimage among men that they may come to you on foot, on every lean camel, and from every deep defile, that they may behold that which is of benefit to them and on indicated days pronounce the name of God over the domestic animals with which He has provided them. So eat thereof and feed him who is wretched and poor.'"[2]

It is clear from the foregoing that the pilgrimage is not only for the wealthy but also for the poor. They all cry, "Here am I, O God, here am I!" They arrive on foot and "on every lean one", that is to say on every lean camel or horse; they come "from every deep defile", or from remote distances. The phrase "over the domestic animals with which we have provided them" refers to the victims and that which is sacrificed during the pilgrimage. "So eat thereof", you who are rich and can afford to make the sacrifice; "and feed him who is wretched and poor": him who has nothing either to eat or to offer up. By "let them put an end to the neglect of their persons"[3] is meant that the pilgrims should shave their heads and trim their nails after putting off the state of *ihram* (tabu).[4] "Let them fulfil their vows" means that if anyone has made a vow to be fulfilled in the land of the pilgrimage, he must accomplish it while he is there. "Let them circumambulate the ancient house" refers to the Ka'bah, to which they turn when they pray.

This is what God has enjoined upon men. It was the duty of Abraham (upon him be peace!), and will be the duty of his successors in the land of the pilgrimage, in the places of devotion, and in the sacred groves, to keep the sacred house clean for those who make the circumambulation, for visitors, and for those who

[2] Koran 22:27–29. The "house" referred to is the Ka'bah at Mecca.
[3] This and the following are commentaries on Koran 22: 30.
[4] The ritual state in which the pilgrim must be in order to perform the sacrifice. See Koran 2:192.

kneel and prostrate themselves in prayer therein. Such was the duty which God has laid upon them, did they but know it.

In the beginning of the Chapter of the Table, in the Koran, God laid down His commands concerning the pilgrimage and covenants, saying, "O ye who believe, fulfil your covenants! Domestic animals are lawful for you with the exception of those about which you have been told; the chase is unlawful for you while you are in a state of tabu, for God decrees what He wills."[5] This means that you shall not engage in hunting while in a state of tabu from the beginning of the pilgrimage until you have completed it and left the limits of the sacred precinct. God said also, "O ye who believe! Do not profane the rites of God or the sacred month" – by detracting from its sacred character by doing that which is unseemly; "or the sacrifice" – that portion of the pilgrimage which is dedicated to the Ka'bah; "or the garlands" – that is to say, the garlands which are placed upon the sacrifice; "or those who visit the sacred house" – referring to the pilgrims and those who visit the Ka'bah throughout the year, who are not to be vexed by taking or plundering their goods or imposing taxes on them, for "they seek grace from God and His approval." The words "When you have put off the state of tabu then hunt, but do not be led into transgression by ill-will against those who have turned you away from the sacred mosque" refer to a turning-away such as takes place at the present day; "but help one another in benevolence and piety and not in sin and wrongdoing. So fear God, for His punishment is severe" means that hate or aversion to those who turn people away from the sacred mosque should not drive one to wrongdoing in breaking the commands of God and acting unjustly. For the pilgrimage is God's and the pilgrims are guests of God. Those who preside over the sacred precinct are the trustees of God, and their task is an important one. God (may He be exalted and glorified!) has said, "We offered the trust to the heavens, the earth, and the mountains, but they refused to accept it and shrank from it; but man took it upon himself – he was unjust and ignorant."[6]

I mention this in the hope that those who oversee the pilgrimage at the present time will make known the necessary payments and taxes they have imposed so that people will not undertake the pilgrimage and return without having discharged their duty to God, even though they have almost reached their goal. It is fitting,

[5] Koran 5:1.
[6] Koran 33:72.

apropos of the present situation, to reproduce here a petition presented to me by some Moroccan pilgrims who reached Jordan but were prevented by their poverty from entering the Hijaz; they did this in the hope that I would intercede with His Majesty King 'Abd al-'Aziz Al Sa'ud. I have reproduced also the fraternal request which I sent to His Majesty and his reply thereto – may God illuminate his perception and guide him to what is right! I do this because of the Prophet's saying that "He who knows something and keeps it hidden God on the day of Resurrection will put a bit[7] of fire in his mouth."

Telegram Addressed to Me by the Moroccan Pilgrims
To His Majesty King 'Abdallah, Amman:
Sire, we are pilgrims from Morocco who have been prevented from making the pilgrimage because of our inability to pay the pilgrimage dues; this has happened after we have travelled thousands of miles and undergone terrifying experience. We implore Your Majesty by the sacred house and by your great ancestor[8] to intercede with the Saudi authorities to permit us to make the pilgrimage before it is too late. May God grant you honour and through you protect His sacred and holy places.

On behalf of fifty Moroccan pilgrims,
Muhammad 'Ali al-Dakali al-Husayn ibn Hasan

Amman, 5 September 1950

My Telegram to His Majesty King 'Abd al-'Aziz
I submit to Your Majesty the entreaties of some Moroccan pilgrims in the above telegram and trust that you will give their case sympathetic consideration.

'Abdallah.

Amman, 6 September 1950

His Majesty's Reply
I have received Your Majesty's kind telegram. Your Majesty my brother knows that nothing gives me greater pleasure than smoothing the path of those making the pilgrimage to the sacred house of God. You know also that the dues which are demanded of the pilgrims are for payment of the guides in the circumambulation of the Ka'bah and other

[7] A bit such as is put in the mouth of a horse.
[8] The Prophet Muhammad.

things – for transportation, and to secure lodging for the pilgrims. If these pilgrims are able to pay their own way, remunerate those who render them services, and take care of their return expenses so as not to be stranded, as has happened previously to others like them, then they will be welcomed with affection and consideration. Otherwise their case is in the hands of God and themselves.

'Abd al-'Aziz

al-Riyad, 6 September 1950

The Virtues of Jerusalem

The position of the Arab states with regard to the internationalization of Jerusalem is a strange one and runs counter to the firm stand previously taken by every Muslim state that had assumed responsibilities in the service of the Holy City.

The Muslim conquest of Jerusalem[9] had a very sacred significance and the Muslims were most careful to preserve the peace; they did not enter the land in order to make trouble. Abu 'Ubaydah 'Amir ibn al-Jarrah (may God be pleased with him!), who was commander of the Muslim army at the time, wrote to the Commander of the Believers, the Caliph 'Umar ibn al-Khattab, that the Patriarch of Jerusalem agreed to surrender the city, but only to 'Umar ibn al-Khattab himself; 'Umar agreed with pleasure and went personally to Palestine. The entry of the Muslim army into Jerusalem was accomplished peacefully and 'Umar recognized all the religious and church rights of the Christian community. When the time for prayer came he was in the Church of the Holy Sepulchre, but he went out beyond the confines of the church and prayed on the spot where the mosque of 'Umar[10] now stands, fearing that otherwise the Muslims might turn the church into a praying-place on the grounds that 'Umar had prayed in it.

From that day to this, no Muslim ruler has governed Palestine without upholding and preserving the covenant made by 'Umar. No Muslim will ever forget Saladin and the Muslim princes and rulers both before and after him who vied with each other to preserve this great honour. How, then, could the states of the Arab League advocate internationalization? It is a strange business and a course that fills one with misgivings. But Jordan's position today is the same as it has been since the days of 'Umar: a sacred chain that

[9] This took place in the year 638.
[10] Not to be confused with the Dome of the Rock.

binds us with its conditions and imposes certain duties upon us. As I dictate these words my eyes and ears are turned toward the Jordanian delegation which has gone to Lake Success[11] to participate in the discussion of the Jerusalem question; my heart is in my mouth, for I fear that I might encounter more difficulty from the Arab states than from the foreign states. However, the die is cast and admonitions and warnings are wasted on people who do not believe.

The sanctity of the mosque of al-Aqsa, for him who wishes to inform himself on this point, is clearly indicated in the Chapter of the Night Journey in the Koran, in the injunctions, commands, guidance, sayings, and lessons which it contains; it is illustrated also by the unimpeachable traditions which I shall presently quote. God willing, this will enable me to overcome every difficulty and task with which I may be confronted. Nevertheless, I hope that I shall be able to work hand in hand with our sister Arab states.

I shall quote here some sayings of the Prophet on the virtues of Jerusalem, following which I shall recite some of the merits of Mecca and Medina both to emphasize my point and to benefit him who is studying the question, for people have almost forgotten what it is their duty to know about these three mosques.

Among the sayings of the Prophet there is one which says, "There are only three mosques to which you should journey: the sacred mosque,[12] this mosque of mine,[13] and the mosque of al-Aqsa."[14] Also, the Imam 'Ali ibn Abi Talib (may God be pleased with him!) is said to have declared that "Jerusalem is the centre of the universe and the closest point on earth to heaven." Abu Hurayrah[15] said, "To die in Jerusalem is as good as dying in heaven."

The Imam 'Ali (may God ennoble his face!) said, "The most blessed of abodes is Jerusalem, and he who lives therein is like one who strives in the way of God. The time will surely come when it will be said, 'O that I were a piece of straw in one of the bricks of Jerusalem!'" It is related that 'Imran ibn Husayn[16] once said, "I asked the apostle of God what the best of cities was. He replied that it was Jerusalem, since its inhabitants did not visit but were visited

[11] The date here is probably December 1949.
[12] In Mecca.
[13] The Prophet's mosque in Medina.
[14] In Jerusalem.
[15] A companion of the Prophet.
[16] Another companion of the Prophet.

and souls were given to it while it did not give its soul to others."
Abu Hurayrah also has reported the Prophet as saying, "Four of the
cities of Paradise are: Mecca, Medina, Damascus, and Jerusalem."[17]

The Virtues of Mecca

Mecca is the sacred of God. By "sacred" (*haram*) it is meant that
all strife, wrongdoing, and worship of other than the one God, the
Judge, the Merciful, the Compassionate, is forbidden within its
bounds. As the noble Koran says,[18] "It is the first house that was
established for mankind", the word "house" signifying one of the
houses of God in which His name is recited and in which He is
praised by men who are not distracted by trade and commerce from
the remembrance of His name. It is the one city in the whole world
that has well-defined limits within which animals may not be
hunted, trees may not be pruned, and in which a fugitive can take
refuge without fear. Furthermore, no one can enter it unless he dons
the *ihram*.[19] This means that he puts off the garments of this world in
order to remove himself from sin and withdraw from the raiment of
luxury and display. In this garb rich and poor are equal; each wears
his seamless garment around his middle and wraps himself in his
mantle, leaving his head bare.

Within the city's confines he kills no game, sheds no blood, and
uses no unseemly language. He puts on the raiment of perfection
and enters the city as a follower of the true religion who professes
the unity of God, selling himself to God and taking leave of his sins.
After circumambulating the house of God and running between
al-Safa and al-Marwah[20] his state of tabu is ended and he enters a
state of divinely-given tranquillity. While in the city he worships
and praises God; then he returns to his homeland ennobled by virtue
of the fact that he has fulfilled one of the five principal duties of
Islam.[21]

We Muslims believe that in Mecca is the ancient house of God,
that it was there that Adam and Eve came together, and that in it are

[17] This section concludes with a list of nine works on the virtues (*fada'il*) of the
city of Jerusalem. They have been omitted from the translation.

[18] Koran 3:90.

[19] See above, p. 65.

[20] For these rites see P. K. Hitti, *History of the Arabs*, 5th ed., New York, 1951,
pp. 133–134.

[21] The five "pillars" of Islam are: prayer, the profession of faith, almsgiving,
fasting, and the pilgrimage. See Hitti, op cit. pp. 130–134.

the place of Abraham and the home and burial-place of Ishmael. To us it is also the city of the tribe of Quraysh and of Muhammad, where the Koran was first revealed; it was the chief city of the Arabs in the days of ignorance before Islam, and it was their pride under Islam. It is God's city and its people belong to God. Concerning them God (may He be glorified and exalted!) has said, "Fighting in it[22] is a great sin, but turning people away from the path of God and disbelief in Him and in the sacred mosque and driving people from it are greater sins in God's eyes."[23] God's anger is upon those who drive them out and molest them.

The Virtues of Medina

In Medina, the Illuminated, is the tomb of the Apostle of God (may God bless him and grant him peace!). It is the place to which he fled from Mecca and from which he defeated the polytheists at Badr,[24] and extirpated them at Uhud.[25] From Medina also God repulsed the confederates;[26] it was the base from which Khaybar was conquered and from which raids were launched and expeditions sent forth. It was there that Islam first gained self-assurance, struck root, and gained its first victories. It is the chief city of Islam, and as the Apostle of God (may God bless him and grant him peace!) said, "Medina is a goodly thing for the Muslims, did they but realize it." Medina is the shrine of the Prophet as Mecca is the shrine of Abraham, upon him be peace! Here are to be found the tombs of Abu Bakr, 'Uthman, al-Hasan, Fatimah, and the great women of early Islam, together with the cemetery of Muhammad's family at al-Baqi.

These are the beliefs which we Muslims hold, and even though these shrines and resting-places may be destroyed the sanctity of Medina will remain and will be well remembered in spite of those who are envious and ignorant. These, then, are the two sacred cities together with a short description of their merits. For him who wishes to go into the subject further there are many well-known works he can consult.

---

[22] One of the three months during which a truce was supposed to prevail.
[23] Koran 2:214.
[24] The first decisive victory of the Muslims, won over the pagan Meccans in 624.
[25] The battle of Uhud (fought in 625) was a victory for the Meccans rather than for the Muslims. The Prophet was wounded in this encounter.
[26] A group of Meccans and their allies who opposed the Muslims.

71

An Appeal to the Muslims

I cannot refrain from addressing a word of exhortation to the Islamic world. I urge the Muslims to stand together as brothers for the right, to be zealous for each other, to respect their convictions and act according to them, and to cling to and fulfil their religious duties. When they do this they will experience peace, happiness, and stability. God (may He be praised and exalted!) has described the Muslims as brethren and has said that they should not domineer over each other. In the Chapter of the Chambers, God in His cherished Book forbade the Muslims to give heed to the reports of disreputable persons: "O you who believe! If a disreputable person brings you information treat it with caution, lest you smite a people without knowing what you are doing and then regret what you have done."[27] Since not all the Arabs at that time were believers He said, "Know that among you is the Apostle of God; if he were to obey you in many things he would become perverse. But God has made faith beloved by you and has made it seemly in your hearts": that is, you have done His bidding and have been saved from transgression. "He has caused you to abhor unbelief, wrongdoing, and disobedience; such are those who follow the right path."[28] The verses which follow declare that "The believers are brothers, so make peace between your two brethren and fear God, that you may receive mercy . . . And if two parties of believers fight between themselves then make peace between them; and if one of them oppresses the other then combat the oppressor until he does God's bidding."[29]

This sets forth the duties of believers toward each other and the divine commands which they should take unto themselves and believe in; it is their duty to be zealous in the execution of these commands and to be guided by them.

It is well known that there is a difference between the believers of today and those of the past. The latter dedicated themselves to God and the faith and were victorious; in recent days the Muslims have forgotten and deviated from this. "So remind, for reminding will benefit the believers."[30] If the people of Islam do not return to their right way and adhere to their virtues they will come to a bad end. The only thing that is suitable for the people of Islam is that which

---

[27] Koran 49:6.
[28] Koran 49:7.
[29] Koran 49:10, 9.
[30] Koran 51:55.

suited the early Muslims. God is our patron and He is a good one to trust in.

The Arab Legion

I should like to add to this Supplement to my memoirs a word about the Arab Legion, the nucleus of which was formed in Amman in 1920.[31] This took place at the time I arrived in Amman following the fall of the Hashimite kingdom of Damascus under the blows of General Gouraud, an event which was hastened also by the political hesitations that afflicted our men in Damascus and rendered them confused and incapable. It was then that the cause was lost.

This nucleus of the Arab Legion was composed of officers and men endowed with a great sense of honour and with courage. Some of them, including Hamid Bey al-Wadi (Hamid Pasha) and Dawud Bey al-Midfa'i, had come with me from the Hijaz. In Ma'an we found 'Abd al-Qadir Bey al-Jundi ('Abd al-Qadir Pasha), Ghalib Bey al-Sha'lan (Ghalib Pasha – may God have mercy on him!), and twenty-five other officers, in addition to 250 enlisted men. This group left Ma'an for Amman and together with the mobile forces there laid the foundation for this army. When policy decreed a soft instead of a tough attitude toward France in Syria it was decided to call this army the Arab Army. Every Arab officer in the Ottoman forces in Syria, Lebanon, and Palestine was given the opportunity to rally to its banner and serve in it. Iraqis and Hijazis also formed part of the original complement of this army, which the British called the Arab Legion. Its training was undertaken by British as well as Arab officers; at the head of these was Colonel Peake Pasha, then a Bey.

I thank God that I am able to say that I owe the greatest share of my success to this army, which does not disgrace its leaders, discourage its commanders, disappoint its people, or shirk or flinch from the defence of either its own rights or those of its country. It is courageous and intrepid as well as obedient and faithful to its orders. With fearlessness and high morale it crushed a revolt in al-Kurah in the north, put down a movement of disaffection in al-Balqa', and established security in the districts of al-Karak, Ma'an, and particularly in Wadi Musa and its vicinity.[32] This army

---

[31] The account of the organization of the Arab Legion may be found in John Bagot Glubb, *The Story of the Arab Legion*, London, 1948, p. 59ff.

[32] See Philip P. Graves (ed.), *Memoirs of King Abdullah of Transjordan*, London, 1950, pp. 205–206, 230, and Glubb, op. cit. pp. 60–61.

is morally upright; it does not cast a covetous eye on the property of others, nor does it indulge in embezzlement or attack those who seek its protection. Because of this, there have been a not inconsiderable number of men from other Arab lands who have joined it. Each has taken back to his country something of these moral standards and has benefited from what he has learned, as I have indicated in the first part of my memoirs.

At this point I should like to say that the Arab Legion's activities in the defence of Jerusalem, including its heroism in street fighting and the reduction of pill-boxes, remind me of the boldness and gallantry which characterized the early warriors of Islam. There are the actions which the Legion undertook in the defence of Bab al-Wad and al-Latrun in the Triangle proper before support from the Iraqi Army arrived; the Legion's capture of the settlements of Kfar Etsion and Neve Ya'aqov; and the forty-eight hour defence put up at Lydda and al-Ramlah by a lone detachment surrounded by two Jewish brigades, after which it escaped and rejoined the main body of our forces with all its equipment. These things show that it has shed glory not only on Jordan, but on every Arab country and on every Arab who is not blinded by envy and ill-will. To such men the weapons and manpower of the Legion are a source of reassurance.

The National Guard forces have recently been constituted as a supplementary part of this army which contributed to our triumph and which was one of the bounties granted by the Creator, may He be glorified and magnified!

The Arab Legion is an army and only that; the sword and bulwark of the land, the pivot of its strength; it is the voice of its country, the scourge of those who are hostile to it, the pitfall of its enemies, and the apple of its ruler's eye. As it grows so does security increase, and as its experience increases so does its ability to shoulder responsibility. The complete brotherhood and comradeship between the Arabs and the British who make up this army is deserving of thanks and praise.

I acknowledge the good work done by our British ally in providing us with needed arms and ammunition; this has always been true except during the period of the Palestine fighting, which is now past. I do not exaggerate if I say that whenever this army is called into the field to come to grips with any adversary, by God's grace it will be as well prepared as any modern army of equal or even relatively greater size.

Royal Address on Hashimite Jordanian Army Day, 25 May 1949

Valiant Army:

I address these words to you with glory, thanks, and humility to God, praising Him for what He has given, lauding Him for His favours, and thanking Him for the grace which He has bestowed upon you and upon me.

He has distinguished you with the odour of sanctity with which Saladin (may God have mercy on him!) also was graced. You are the true heirs of those who fought under the chosen Prophet and of the others who did battle for the Faith; in bravery, skill, and character you are the descendants of these forefathers. Without ingrained moral strength and obedience and the self-restraint of a devoted soldiery, no victorious army can attain its objectives or fulfil its destiny. Our army is the rampart of the kingdom, the ornament of the people, the arm of authority, and the pride of the land. It will be a strong fortress and an impregnable citadel as long as it possesses the attributes of manliness, courage, and obedience.

I stress this particularly because if an army is morally weak, this malady causes it to decay; if it is morally sound it is free from all such sickness. In my capacity as your chief, mentor, and guide I say that you are the greatest reward which God has granted me in this life, and I praise and thank Him for it.

An army with this moral character can enable its people and their government to win in peace as well as in war. Your link with the army of the Prophet lies in your relationship to me. The Prophet's army that fought victoriously at Badr was the nucleus which gave rise to Arab armies that made their conquests, established the Arab civilization, and continued developing in strength and loyalty until they reached their apogee in the era of the Orthodox Caliphs, the Umayyads, and the Abbasids. This was followed by an interval during which the East was served by other armies of their brethren belonging to the Muslim sultans – may God have mercy on them! – who neither shirked nor hung back from their duty. Finally the army of the Prophet was revived, as is well known, by the awakener of his Arab people, the Commander of the Believers[33] al-Husayn ibn 'Ali, may God be pleased with him!

I hope that you will be the best descendants of such forefathers and that you will preserve your moral character and bring back the glories of the past. God willing, this will lead to a general Syrian unity, which was one of the foundations of the blessed Arab Revolt, and thence to a general unification of the Arabs.

[33] This caliphal title is used since King Husayn assumed the dignity of that office in 1924.

The reputation which you enjoy is a source of pride and glory to me. Accept my congratulations and my sincere prayers that God may make you the apple of your country's eye and the pivot of its power and splendour. I ask God's mercy on your martyred dead and hope for the best for you.

Chapter 4
Lest We Forget

Palestine

*The following are official memoranda which His Hashimite Majesty –
at that time His Royal Highness the Amir – transmitted to the High
Commissioner in Palestine a number of years before the advent of the great
tragedy in that country. If they reveal anything, it is a penetrating sagacity,
an unerring insight, and a deep devotion to the Arab cause. They reveal also
the shortsightedness of the leaders of the Arab movement in Palestine, who
because they turned a deaf ear to the Hashimite counsel, guidance, and
warning were overwhelmed by the calamity the woes and evils of which we
are still suffering.*

*The reader will note that His Majesty was the first to prophesy to the
Arabs of Palestine that they would suffer dispersal and destruction if they
continued in their mistaken policy. He was also the first to warn them of the
evil fate they would suffer if they persisted in relying on "weeping and
wailing" and seeking help from those who "have no power either to harm
them or to help them."[1] In the letter sent by His Majesty to the late Dr 'Abd
al-Hamid Sa'id the reader will find a piece of sound foresight. The myth
that "the Muslim and Arab worlds are gathering their forces and will fight
for us" had come to dominate the minds and hearts of the Palestine Arabs,
but when the time came to gather the forces and come to their aid nothing was
forthcoming but neglect, false promises, and failure.*

*We regret bitterly the neglect of our national duty which we committed in
failing to give heed to the counsels of the great ruler and pillar of the pure
Hashimite house. May those who are wise take this as an example.*

Protest against Large-scale Jewish Immigration into Palestine
To His Excellency the High Commissioner for Transjordan.[2]
Dear Excellency:

I have learned of your return to Jerusalem and I trust that Your

---

[1] Koran 5:80, etc. The reference is to the Prophet's exhorting the Arabs on the
futility of turning to their impotent pagan deities.

[2] Sir Arthur Wauchope, High Commissioner for Palestine and Transjordan.

77

Excellency is safe and well. Once more I send you my felicitations and I thank you for writing me before your departure. I assure you that my brother His Majesty King 'Ali,[3] regarding whom you particularly inquired, is enjoying very good health, thanks to God, and he has charged me with thanking Your Excellency for your interest and friendly feelings.

I cannot conceal my pleasure at the wisdom with which matters were handled in Palestine during the recent strike resulting from large-scale immigration to Palestine from Germany in particular and from other countries in general. In this regard I feel it incumbent on me to explain to you something of what is going on in the minds of the Arabs.

The Arabs in Palestine are convinced that the Jews wish to exploit the misfortune of their expulsion from Germany to speed up the execution of their well-known desire to Judaize Palestine. They have revealed their hidden intentions with a recklessness that has exhausted the Arabs' patience. The Arabs see themselves daily under attack by people who have been cast out of other countries and whom Palestine is obliged to receive and welcome. Palestine is obliged also to accept the customs and *mores* brought by these immigrants, which are not in conformity with the holy character of the country. I do not think it strange *if there has arisen in the minds of the Arabs, both Muslim and Christian, the idea that they are in danger of being extinguished and on the verge of being destroyed* by these intruders pouring in on them from all directions. This is especially understandable since they have seen a great people like the Germans, who are well organized and highly civilized and developed, fearing for their existence and homeland because of the Jews who have remained strangers in their midst even though they have lived among the Germans for many centuries and have ties of language, blood, and interest with them. How can one blame the Arabs, who had been suffering the trials and tribulations inherited from past generations and were on the point of believing that the armistice after World War I would usher in a new dawn of peace, for being taken aback by this overwhelming Jewish immigration?

Many intelligent Arabs have declared to me that after the Germans began expelling the Jews their fears increased daily lest other countries should follow suit; in such an event, what would become of the Arabs of Palestine? How could they ward off this calamity of having to receive from other countries Jews with first-class European educations in science, the professions, and in the mechanical and military fields, like the German Jews who were indisputably skilled in all these fields and competent in others as well? In addition, the Arabs believed that the reports of experts sent to Palestine by the British Government agreed with the Arabs' views

[3] Ex-king of the Hijaz, in exile since 1925.

and complaints on many points, but nothing was ever changed and matters remained as they were.

In a previous letter to the High Commissioner's office dated on the first of Jumada I AH 1348 (15 October 1929) I stated that Palestine was due for a number of surprises. I said that the Jews were increasing their competition with the Arabs and that they were adding many problems to that of the National Home.

Motivated as I am by a desire for genuine co-operation and wishing to do my duty as a neighbour sharing the common interest, I have no alternative but to speak my thoughts. Therefore I repeat today what I said yesterday, adding that the nationalism kindled in the breasts of these peoples following World War I is the cause of these demonstrations and strikes and the events which have resulted from them. In addition to the spirit that has moved the Arabs of Palestine to take such action *there is a fear of extermination which has begun to appear in various parts of the country in a disturbing fashion*. It is threatening also the neighbouring Arab countries, which regard this tragedy with deep distress which tomorrow could develop into an emotion that might rupture the peace and cost the government a great deal of trouble and treasure.

I do not despair of finding the means to repel these dangers. I may say that the time has already come to bring about reasonable and speedy solutions to these problems. Even if they should not all be acceptable they will at least reassure people's minds and prepare them for agreement.

I trust that through Your Excellency's mediation my words will be accepted by the august British Government in the sense intended by me, who am motivated by a desire for the welfare and peace of Palestine and my neighbouring country. For my country has begun to be affected by the ideas and fears current in Palestine, as have the adjoining Arab countries and the British Government, to which I am linked by the bonds of genuine friendship and past memories of a common struggle which cannot be forgotten.

Accept, Sir, my best greetings and highest respect.

Your Excellency's sincere friend, 'Abdallah

Amman, 29 Jumada II 1352 (18 October 1933)

A Statement of the Fears of the Palestine Arabs

His Excellency the High Commissioner for Transjordan[4]

Dear Excellency:

As a personal friend of Your Excellency who is aware of the heavy burdens you are bearing; as the son of your World War ally whose armies were of active assistance in the Palestine theatre as stated by the Colonial Secretary[5] in a speech delivered at a dinner for me in London on 26 June 1934; as ruler of an Arab country bordering on Palestine; as a Muslim and a descendant of the Prophet who is near to the Holy Places of Palestine and particularly its mosque of al-Aqsa; as a leader who bears not a small share of responsibility for the Arab Revolt; and as one who sees the state which his fellow Arabs in Palestine have attained, I find myself compelled to speak in the following free and frank manner:

1. I understand from His Excellency the Colonial Secretary that His Majesty's Government has placed complete trust in the person of Your Excellency and that you are the sole authority upon which it relies in the Palestine question. Appreciating as I do the gravity of this responsibility I cannot conceal my pleasure at this news because of my confidence in the good understanding and firm bonds of friendship that exist between your honourable person and myself. I am aware also that you have an unfettered love of justice and a genuine discrimination for those things which link the interests of your noble government and people with the Arabs as opposed to others in the Near East.

With regard to the idea prevalent among us Arabs that the Jews in Great Britain enjoy a privileged position because some of their leaders occupy high posts in the government and in the House of Commons and thus are able to direct British policy along lines completely favourable to their own people rather than to others, I have learned also from His Excellency the Colonial Secretary that this is not the case and that it is an erroneous belief. He has reassured me that on the contrary the British Government is not so influenced and that it follows a just course of action and one which is in accord with its national traditions.

For this and other reasons which I have already set forth I have deemed it fitting to write to Your Excellency on the subject of the Arab cause in Palestine, since any further delay would be reckoned as a grave disregard on my part of the national right of both the Arabs and their British friends.

2. The Arabs are greatly distressed because they perceive no concrete results from the reports of the British missions which in past years have

[4] Sir Arthur Wauchope.

[5] This probably refers to Sir Philip Cunliffe-Lister, who was Colonial Secretary from 9 November 1931 to 6 June 1935.

been sent to Palestine to inquire into the true state of affairs there. This is in spite of the importance of their testimony and despite the truths contained in the White Paper[6] issued by former Colonial Secretary Lord Passfield.

3. The promises made to the Arabs during the World War were anterior to and more precise than the Balfour Declaration. It was these promises which moved a great many Palestinians – soldiers, officers, and civilians – to desert from the Turkish Army and rally to the banner of my father King Husayn in the Arab Revolt, during which its heroes fought side by side with the British forces. At that time the Zionists had absolutely no political position in Palestine and in no way constituted an element of its population.

4. The joint declaration issued in November 1918 by the two allied powers of Great Britain and France specifically stated that the Arabs would not be compelled to accept any form of government not agreeable to them. On the contrary, it was said that they would encourage the establishment of Arab national governments and that they would extend to them the assistance necessary for their consolidation and success.[7] This declaration should be granted the importance it deserves and it should be taken into account when considering the carrying-out of the Balfour Declaration in Palestine.

5. The Balfour Declaration provides that the Jews should have a national home in Palestine. The indications, however, are that *the Jews by various means and without opposition have been able to devise a programme for turning all of Palestine into a national home for the Jews.* If any impartial observer were to compare their position at the beginning of the immigration into Palestine with the great progress they have made up to the present in colonizing the country, *he would say that their success has been almost complete and that they will attain their goal in a few years.*

6. The Balfour Declaration lays down the condition that the interests of the Arab inhabitants are not to be harmed; in other words, that the interests of the Arabs are to be protected in their entirety. The Arabs, however, see a manifest threat to their existence in the steady Jewish immigration into Palestine accompanied by an influx of illegal arrivals in flagrant violation of this promise. In addition, the fears of the Arab political leaders are supported by the fact that the sale of land continues unrestricted and every day one piece of land after another is torn from the hands of the Arabs.

I know that this cannot be completely stopped even by the use of force.

[6] This was issued in 1930 as the result of an investigation into the causes of the disturbances of 1929. It appeared as Cmd. 3530.

[7] This citation differs considerably from the text of the Anglo–French declaration of 7 November 1918 as reproduced in George Antonius, *The Arab Awakening*, London, 1938, p. 436.

Nevertheless, I draw Your Excellency's attention to the difficult situation in which the Arabs find themselves in the face of the strong organization of the Zionists. In such cases it would be governments which would prevent the disappearance and submerging of a people. If these people possessed representatives in parliamentary or legislative bodies, they would be able to play their part in defending the people and countering the danger that threatens them.

7. Protection of the weak was one of the most honourable of the high aims for which the last World War was fought. What is more worthy of this noble principle than to remember it in times of peace in connection with the situation of the Palestine Arabs who made sacrifices in the war at a time when they were masters of their own country and without rivals for control of it?

8. The Jewish immigration has brought to Palestine incompatible peoples of different principles and outlook from the Arabs, who have brought continual unrest and trouble to this peaceful and holy land. *Furthermore, Palestine has become a potential source of social danger the enormity of which will become apparent as soon as world peace is again disturbed*; this corruption will spread to the Arab countries in particular and to the Near East in general. I do not believe that the Government of Palestine would come to any different conclusion if it were to make a profound study of the situation; this is supported by the nature of certain clandestine Jewish groups the existence of which has been revealed by the law-courts.

9. The Jews have attempted and continue to attempt to go beyond the promises made in the Balfour Declaration and thereby have given rise in the minds of the Arabs to a fixed idea that *a Jewish state is being created which is masquerading under the name of the National Home*. The implications of this are causing fears to spread to the Arab countries outside of Palestine and to those persons in these countries who are in positions of important responsibility. The Jews have never given the slightest indication of their ability to amalgamate with the original Arab inhabitants of the country. I wish from the bottom of my heart that it were otherwise.

10. My experience leads me to believe that if the situation continues as it is, with unrestricted immigration and other things complained of by the Arabs, *it will lead to evil and terrible results in the near future*. I do not feel that at present sufficient thought is being given to this possibility; matters are being dealt with on a day-to-day basis. As a result of this it is still said that there is room for new immigrants and that there is land which can be sold. Nevertheless, I hope that Your Excellency will join me in giving thought to the future we may face, and to the problems that may be most difficult to solve if immigration and the sale of land continue.

Your Excellency:

I lay before Your Excellency these matters which have disturbed the Arabs both in and out of Palestine. If I have told Your Excellency that the Muslim world is likewise disturbed by these events it is because I am quite certain that this is so. For this reason I have thought that I should draw Your Excellency's attention to these knotty problems which, with God's permission, I trust will be overcome by you.

I do not deny that Great Britain's interests have expanded in Palestine and the Arab countries since the war. But do you not feel, as I do, that in view of all this the continuation of the genuine friendship which the Arabs feel for your noble nation is an essential thing that must be nurtured and preserved?

Both in the past and in the present I have done all in my power to support these ties between the two nations. This is because I firmly believe that it is in the interest of the Arabs as well as the English to do so. I do not deny that my Arab people in Palestine have fallen into a number of political errors, but in my opinion this is all due to their overwhelming fear that their existence is being threatened. It is not to be expected, of course, that a people who are in such a state should preserve their normal balanced frame of mind or think as calmly as they ought to. For this reason their mistakes should be overlooked since the reasons for them are all too apparent.

I communicate to you in all frankness the fears of my Arab people in Palestine and I have summed them up in this memorandum to the best of my ability. It is my hope that you will consider this as an assistance from me to Your Excellency in the performance of the difficult duty which you have undertaken and will see it as motivated by sincere friendship for both my Arab people and my British friends.

Accept, Excellency, my highest esteem and my best greetings.

Your Excellency's sincere friend, 'Abdallah

Amman, 25 July 1934.

A Defence of the Arabs in the 1936 Revolt

My dear Sir Arthur Wauchope:

It is some time since I have communicated with you, partly because I did not wish to complicate matters and partly because I wished to observe the course of events.

Several evenings ago I heard the radio address which you delivered and I sensed in it the goodness of your intention and your desire for the general welfare. I regret that others, unlike myself, have failed to perceive and understand its intended object, as is indicated both by what has been written in the press and by the information which has reached me. You well know that my previous communications to you have been both friendly as well as official and that they contained my views on what should be done by you to deal with the Palestine problem. My greatest object in this has been that you should succeed and that the Arabs should be secure in their homeland, but I have not sought to deprive the Jews of what they have gained for themselves. This message, however, is a purely personal one; it has no official character and is devoid of anything inspired or called forth by my own sympathies.

First of all I must assure Your Excellency that the situation is daily becoming more serious and that the Arabs who in Palestine are defending their homeland and their race are prepared to continue doing so until they are either annihilated or saved. God alone knows the trouble it is costing me to preserve peace in Transjordan with cries from Palestine daily rending the ears of my people, while disturbing news circulates among them and zealots seek to stir them up through religious and racial agitation.

You must have heard of the conference presided over by Mithqal ibn Fayiz which was held in the village of Umm al-'Amad[8] before I learned about it and which was participated in by nearly all the sheikhs of the country. I prevented its organizers from rallying the sheikhs lest they stir up a tension which would have led to results that I did not desire for the sake of their own safety. I hoped also that wisdom in dealing with the Palestine problem would prevail in the end. From the activity of this Transjordanian conference Your Excellency will perceive the degree of popular impatience and agitation resulting from almost three months' deadlock between the Arabs and the government over the problem.

I should like to explain to Your Excellency something of the Arab character and state of mind. The increased use of military force has caused the growth of desperation among the people. I do not doubt that after studying the situation you have been convinced that military action is useful. But military action is only for the purpose of overcoming and expelling the known enemy. The most effective solution of the difficulties arising among these elements is to establish in the minds of the people the reassuring conviction that these problems will be justly and impartially dealt with in an open fashion so that they will be able to see with their own eyes the government's desire concretely expressed in combating calamity and removing the cause for complaint.

[8] This village lies about twelve miles south of Amman on the road to Ma'daba and is the birthplace of Mithqal Pasha al-Fayiz (or al-Fa'iz), shaykh of the al-Fa'iz sub-tribe of the Banu Sakhr. Here on 2 July 1936 Mithqal Pasha called a congress of Transjordanian notables and their followers who vigorously expressed their sympathy for the Palestine Arabs and called for a *jihad* on their behalf. See *Oriente Moderno*, 1936, p. 467.

I can assure you without the slightest hesitancy that tolerance and clemency are not looked upon by the Arabs as weakness; on the contrary, they are considered an indication of justice, wisdom, and political competence in the conduct of affairs. Palestine complains of Jewish immigration and its tyranny, but it has not said that it wants to expel those Jews who have entered up to the present time. If their immigration should continue against the will of the Arabs and without the Arabs – the original inhabitants of the country – being consulted, you would be justified in demanding a thoroughgoing investigation by the Royal Commission.[9]

In this respect I should like to draw your attention to the degree in which the Arabs' confidence in this Royal Commission has changed. Propaganda against it grows more intense as time passes and I fear that all hope in it will disappear. Inevitably this will end in bloodshed and the destruction of homes, in atrocities and terrors which can be avoided with beforehandedness and forbearance and by reassuring those who are afraid and agitated. Or alternatively, Your Excellency could take over the task of the Commission itself as Lord Allenby[10] did in Egypt, thereby rescuing both Egypt and the British Government from a difficult situation which certainly would have become much more aggravated had it not been for his efforts, which found a solution for the Egyptian crisis at its most critical point. Great Britain's position was not damaged thereby nor was she charged with weakness in the face of force; one can see the fruits of this effort which are being gathered today.

Public opinion in Palestine and Transjordan is unanimous. I am working night and day to preserve a policy of peace in Transjordan, as well as to prevent there an explosion which I fear will not be long delayed if the turmoil in Palestine either continues or degenerates into war. This I say from certain knowledge. In recalling the frightening possibilities I have alluded to earlier in this letter of mine, I do not forget the decision of the Palestine court which has increased the belief of the people everywhere in the justice of their cause and has convinced them that they are defending the right which is entirely on their side. The views of the Arab government officials have been made clear to Your Excellency by their memorandum to you. Their disaffection is spreading to the officials here in Transjordan, whose sympathy for their Palestinian colleagues is growing continually stronger.

I beg you to read this letter of mine over carefully and consider it as advice from one brother to another. I only say that when you look at the ruins spread throughout this unfortunate country they bear eloquent

[9] This refers to the Peel Commission of 1936–1937. For its report see Cmd. 5479.
[10] Allenby took over as High Commissioner in a troubled Egypt on 25 March 1919.

testimony to the effects of repression and military action by various states throughout history. They reveal also that the forefathers and ancestors of the Arabs have handed these possessions down to them from the past and that they have become dear and familiar to them.

The Arabs in no way expected this treatment which they received from the British Government. They considered that Britain, unlike previous governments, had another way of solving problems, namely, through justice, forbearance, and patience as the British have done in all parts of the East. In short, the Arabs believed that for all this the British had a remedy other than fire and the sword, which never in all their history had been profitable or advantageous to them.

This is the hope which has prevailed among the Arabs up to the present hour in spite of the repressive measures from which they have suffered. It is my eager desire to preserve this faith which leads me to burden you with my letters and communications. In any case, I am motivated solely by a desire to promote the welfare of your people and mine and by my conciliatory and personally friendly feelings towards you. May God preserve you, my dear friend.

Your Excellency's sincere friend, 'Abdallah

Amman, 10 July 1936

A Letter to 'Abd al-Hamid Sa'id

In the name of God the Merciful, the Compassionate;
I praise Him and bless His Prophet, his house, and all his Companions.
From 'Abdallah ibn al-Husayn ibn Ali to 'Abd al-Hamid Bey Sa'id, President of the Young Muslim Men's Association in Cairo:

Peace and the mercy and blessings of God be upon you. To you I praise God, other than whom there is no god, and I bless and pray for the peace of Muhammad, the last of the prophets, and his house and companions.

I have received your letter sent from Cairo on 2 Rabi' II 1357[11] regarding the Palestine problem and the proposal which was inspired by my familiarity with Palestine and by what my proximity to the country has permitted me to see and hear.

Your kind letter was filled with good counsel and sincere feeling for God, His Prophet, the believers, and myself. May God grant you the best of rewards on my behalf, and you can be sure that He will. Here is the truth

[11] 1 June 1938.

86

clearly and fully set forth for you, and after reading it you can draw your own conclusion.

I came to Transjordan in the year 1921[12] after Syria fell into the hands of the French in the manner which is well known to all. God then enabled me to put forth my best effort for the founding of the state of Iraq by my later brother Faysal. He granted me success in creating the government of Transjordan by having it separated from the Balfour Declaration,[13] which had included it since the Sykes-Picot Agreement[14] had assigned it to the British zone of influence.

The first incident between the Jews and the people of Palestine was the one that took place in Jaffa in the spring of 1921. This was followed by a period of calm during which the Balfour Declaration began to be carried out under conditions of complete tranquillity. The late Musa Kazim Pasha al-Husayni was chosen by the Muslims as president of the Palestine Congress[15] and al-Hajj Amin al-Husayni was made Mufti and President of the Supreme Muslim Council in Palestine.

In the meantime the Jews were increasing in numbers and consolidating their influence. In the few years covering the tenure of office of Sir Herbert Samuel, Lord Plumer, Sir John Chancellor, Sir Arthur Wauchope, and Sir Harold MacMichael,[16] the Jews, who in 1921 did not number more than 100,000, had increased to 450,000. They had acquired control of the most fertile portion of the land and had settled in every pass, wadi, plain, and wilderness from Beersheba to Lake Hulah. An Arab could not go from one village to another without seeing a Jewish village separating the two.

So now, my brother in Islam, you see that the pillars of Zionism are three: the Balfour Declaration, the European nations which have decided to expel the Jews from the territories and direct them to Palestine, *and those partisans of the Arabs who will accept no solution but are content with weeping and wailing and calling for help to those who cannot aid them. Thus is Palestine giving up the ghost.*

[12] Actually it was in November 1920.

[13] This is inexact. In fact, the Secretary General of the League of Nations in a note of 23 September 1922 addressed to the members of the League quoted the decision of the Council excepting Transjordan from certain provisions of the Palestine mandate, including Article 6 which provided for facilitation of Jewish immigration and settlement on the land. This was approved by the Council of the League in September 1922.

[14] Concluded in London on 16 May 1916.

[15] It is unclear which Palestine congress is referred to; there were several which were presided over by Musa Kazim, the last being the seventh Palestine Arab Congress held in Jerusalem in June 1928.

[16] These are the High Commissioners of Palestine from 1920 to 1938, the date of this letter.

According to my information the Jews have requested the continuance of the mandate so that they can buy up more land and bring in additional immigrants. No other country has gone through such a trial as Palestine. Egypt's suffering, for example, was under foreign occupation and was remedied by Egypt's demanding its rights and putting an end to unrest, with the result that today Egypt has attained some of its aspirations; the same can be said of Iraq and Syria.

Palestine, however, is threatened with the danger of being overrun by another people. *The remedy for Palestine's malady lies in a speedy halting of the danger and in reducing the attack, then in considering how to put an end to it once and for all. Procrastination will mean the end of Palestine.* I am firmly convinced also that complaining will be of no avail, since the Muslim governments of the East which are members of the League of Nations are unable to do anything effective owing to their well-known long-term treaties with the government that holds the mandate for Palestine. Furthermore, since the people of Palestine have confined themselves to making protests, I have considered it my duty under my religion according to which I worship God and as something enjoined upon me by my ethnic affiliation, to strive to ward off the calamity by bringing about the union of Palestine and Transjordan. The inhabitants of Palestine are 100,000 more than those of Transjordan and would ably take over the leadership of the administration of such a united state. There would be a parliament to represent the people and an army to defend them. Finances would be unified and the shores of the state would be well patrolled and its gates shut to prevent clandestine immigration. The country would have a breathing-spell in which to recuperate, while at the same time its neighbouring sister Eastern countries would be enabled to make not a little progress toward strengthening the bonds and ties between them. This accomplished, they could then deal with the problem on a more long-range basis and with a strengthened hand and a single voice.

These are the reasons which have prompted me to transmit my views to you. I should like to know now whether you have any ideas that are better than those I have set forth. Or are you among those who believe that *there is no harm in continuing the present deleterious mandate despite the Jewish usurpers it has brought and despite the demonstrated inability of those Palestinians now at the political helm to prevent their compatriots from selling their land*? Furthermore, it is made quite clear to all, both by the map drawn up by the Simpson Commission[17] and by another compiled by the Peel Commission,[18] that *the*

[17] Sir John Hope Simpson, *Palestine: Report on Immigration, Land Settlement and Development*, London, 1930. Cmd. 3686.

[18] *Palestine Royal Commission Report*, London, 1937. Cmd. 5479.

Arabs are as prodigal in selling their land as they are in useless wailing and weeping.

If you consider all this carefully your eyes will be opened and you will perceive the painful truth as I do. It has frightened me to behold the general lack of concern for the calamity which is in the making as a result of this taking-over of the country and the continuance of the present state of affairs which will lead to Palestine's becoming entirely Jewish in two years. For this reason I say "O God, guide my people, for they do not know."

Peace and the mercy and blessings of God be upon you.

['Abdallah]

6 Rabi' II 1357 (5 June 1938)

Text of the Proposal for the Solution of the Palestine Problem Sent to the British Government

1. A united Arab kingdom shall be constituted from Palestine and Transjordan under an Arab monarchy capable of conducting its affairs and carrying out its obligations.

2. This kingdom shall provide an elected administration for the Jews in the Jewish districts, which shall be mapped out by a commission composed of British, Arab, and Jewish members.

3. The Jewish administration shall enjoy all the rights and privileges enjoyed by any other administration in the country.

4. In the parliament of this Arab state the Jews shall be represented in proportion to their numbers and shall be permitted to serve as cabinet ministers of the united state.

5. Jewish immigration shall be restricted to a reasonable figure in the territory of the Jewish administration.

6. The Jews shall not have the right to seek to buy land or introduce new immigrants into the area outside the Jewish districts.

7. This arrangement shall prevail for ten years; it shall be tried out for eight years, and in the course of the last two years a final decision shall be taken as to the future, the declaration of the country's independence, and the termination of the mandate.

8. If the Arabs should conclude that the intentions of the Jews are good and that they intend to live together with the Arabs, the Arabs shall have the right to permit the entrance of a suitable number of immigrants into the territories of the unified state if they should wish to do so.

9. During this period the mandate shall continue in a purely supervisory capacity limited to the overseeing and surveillance of the unified state.

10. There shall be no objection to the British Army's remaining during this ten-year period.

11. At the end of the eighth and the beginning of the ninth year it will be the duty of the government and parliament of the unified state to make known the final decision as to the future of the country and to carry out whatever solution may be decided upon.

12. Discussions regarding British interests, such as a projected treaty, shall begin immediately so as to be ready for ratification at the end of the ten years and at the time of the declaration of the country's independence. Projects for general reforms in financial affairs, irrigation, the army, roads, communications, and other state functions shall be carried out in a uniform manner and by a single authority.

L'Envoi

I hope that I have discharged my duty toward my people by speaking out concerning the foregoing truths and affairs, in what I have said about the present-day Arabs, in the general opinions I have set forth, and in the portrayal I have made of my people's thinking. I trust also that both expressly and by implication I have interpreted the aspirations of the people. With the sole object of elevating the status of the Arabs and bringing about a renaissance of Islam I make an appeal for unity, cohesion, and union. I call upon my people to cast off the evildoers and follow men who are good. The only thing that grieves me is the disunity, weakness, and powerlessness which have overwhelmed my people and the error and ignorance that have blinded their eyes. But I firmly expect that victory will be theirs if they plan their case, remember their history, and strengthen their determination.

I have completed this message with sincere faith in God and the right. It is the product of trials, tribulations, and wars, and the fruit of political experience and the contest of battle. If I have succeeded in accomplishing my task I could not wish for more.

'Abdallah ibn al-Husayn

Appendix A[1]

Diploma of Appointment of
His Excellency Raghib Pasha al-Nashashibi
as Overseer of al-Haram al-Sharif and
High Guardian of the Holy Places

From 'Abdallah ibn al-Husayn, by the help of God King of the Hashimite Kingdom of the Jordan, to the most honoured of exemplary and notable men and paragon of those of virtue and importance, executor of the affairs of the religious communities and faiths with keenness of mind and rectitude of thought, who bears all glory and honour and who has previously given evidence of his good character: our Minister and dear friend, wearer of the Order of the Renaissance first class, His Excellency Raghib Pasha al-Nashashibi:

Because of the praiseworthy characteristics which I have observed in your person and because of your hitherto upright conduct, I have proclaimed my Royal Hashimite will that you be appointed to the post of Overseer of al-Haram al-Sharif[2] and High Guardian of the Holy Places, in the hope that you will make fruitful efforts and use an enlightened approach in caring for the Mosque of al-Aqsa, the environs of which have been blessed by God, and that our troops and fighters will be able to restore it to its former state and position as a centre of pilgrimage. I hope also that you will spread the wing of attention and protection over all the religious communities and over the pilgrims of all nations and that you will show the utmost concern for the preservation of their safety, freedom, sanctity, rites, and places of worship. I trust that you will restore everything to its proper place and that in accord with the well-known *status quo* you will see that all religious communities, mosques, churches, and synagogues be given their full rights so that all may be reassured and that peace and harmony may reign. Let the example of the great prophets be followed and let the heavenly faiths be framed with human brotherhood in a holy, Arab city glorified by religious worship, where prayer is offered up and trusts are preserved. In your conduct you should follow the precepts of 'Umar[3]

[1] In the original text these documents immediately follow the Appeal to the Muslims.

[2] The sacred area in Jerusalem in which the Dome of the Rock and the Mosque of al-Aqsa are located.

[3] Caliph 'Umar I (634–644).

92

and the traditions handed down from our forebears in all periods of Islam. You should accept the *firmans* of the Sultans and the official decrees in the possession of the patriarchs, and you should establish the various rights in a fixed and special register and record which may be consulted when necessary and which should be your guide in all matters. You are to follow your upright predecessors in multiplying good deeds and avoiding those which are bad. Put an end to wrongdoing and strengthen the pillars of the community, being guided by the sense of the Koranic verse, "O ye people! We have created you from male and female and have made you into peoples and tribes that you may know one another. Verily, those of you who find most favour with God are the most pious."[4]

May God guide your steps and distinguish you with increasing honour and good fortune; may He grant you blessing, prosperity, and success.

Issued at al-Musalla Palace

27 Rabi' I 1370 (5 January 1951)

Reply of His Excellency Raghib Pasha al-Nashashibi
Your Majesty:

Praise be to God who has inscribed me among your pious followers and has made me a member of your chosen army. I work in the shadow of your guidance, trusting in your protection, continually enjoying your sympathy, and always strengthened by your love and confidence. Praise be to God, who has ornamented my life by associating me with you, who has crowned my existence by joining me with you, who has liberated me by making me obedient to you, who has made me one of your followers, who has made me a true lover of your person, and who has caused me to be a trusted friend of your throne.

It is indeed by the grace and favour of God, Sire, that you have entrusted me with an honour from the wellspring of your favour – the honour that clothes the office of Overseer of al-Haram al-Sharif and High Guardian of the Holy Places, the merit for the preservation of which belongs entirely to you. In this you have set the best of examples, recalling the memory of the most outstanding caliphs of Islam and the best of those companions of the Prophet who worked and fought for the Faith. Indeed, Sire, in the eyes of men of perception this holy and faithful city is more worthy of consideration than any other. To its mosque your great ancestor (upon him be the most gracious of blessings and the most serene peace!), the bearer of the message of Islam, made his night journey,[5] while nearby the

---

[4] Koran 49:13.
[5] The Prophet Muhammad's night journey to Jerusalem; see Koran 17.

apostle of love and concord was born. It has always been a city of revelation and inspiration and a source of light and peace.

Today it regains the glory and power which it enjoyed of yore, for it has found in your valorous army the swift means of repulsing the advancing enemy. It has remained safe, protected by your sympathy, glorified by your presence, and guarded by your great heart. It is understandable, therefore, that you have desired for it a guardian who would seek success from your counsel and strive to spread equality and justice by virtue of your wisdom and in accordance with your views and sound opinions. Weak as I am, I shall take the directives embodied in the high royal diploma as a lamp by which to be guided and a beacon by which to travel. With this I shall be able to overcome difficulties and fulfil the duties arising from my concern with the Holy Places, with equal treatment of the city's various peoples, and with absolute justice among its religious communities. It is a most glorious thing that the Holy Places are today in your Arab Hashimite hands, which are known by the world as tolerant and respectful of the various religious rites. This is your era, Sire; you are its leader and its banners have been raised over this sacred place. May God grant you victory and make your firm throne a beauty-mark on the face of time; and may He facilitate my success in serving you, in giving you selfless affection, and in devoting myself to your person and your throne.

Appendix B

Diploma of Appointment of His Eminence Shaykh Muhammad al-Amin al-Shanqiti as President of the Corps of Ulema in the Hashimite Kingdom of Jordan

To the paragon of the recognized ulema, mine of virtue and steadfast faith, servant of the noble Islamic sciences and the lofty law of Islam, His Eminence the honourable master and President of the Corps of Ulema, Shaykh Muhammad al-Amin al-Shanqiti:

To the pride of the ulema and witness of the virtuous, our former Chief Qadi and most gracious Mufti of Jerusalem, His Eminence Shaykh Husain al-Din Jar Allah; Your eminences and gracious members of the Corps of Ulema:

I praise God for His blessings and favours and I bless and salute the last of His prophets and the lord of His chosen ones and his excellent house and most honoured companions.

Since men and the jinn were created to worship God the High, the Mighty, as He has said (may He be glorified!): "I created the jinn and mankind only in order that they should worship Me";[1] and since strengthening the objectives of the *sharia* law, the divine sciences, and the programme of Islam is one of my most important tasks, I therefore have issued my royal Hashimite *iradah* for the creation of a Corps of Ulema to set a sound example in knowledge and deed and to be a model of wisdom and fear of God (". . . those of God's servants who are wise fear Him"[2]). May they turn to God for understanding ("Say: 'This is my way; I and those who follow me pray to God for understanding' "[3]); may they follow the path of truth, good, teaching, and guidance; may they order the doing of good and forbid the doing of evil; may they give consideration to the people's responsibilities for their happiness in this world and the next and for the victory of the descendants of Hasan[4] (". . . that there may be among you a people who appeal for the good and command that kindness

[1] Koran 51:56.
[2] Koran 35:25.
[3] Koran 12:108.
[4] This refers to the Hashimite House, which claims descent from the Prophet through his grandson al-Hasan.

95

be done, while forbidding that which is evil; these are the ones who will prosper"[5]).

At the present time there are errors which have grown up and many people in their daily lives have substituted worldly for religious precepts to the degree that they have forgotten that knowledge of God is the object of their creation and they neglect the obligations of the people of Muhammad (may God bless him and grant him peace!). Therefore, in accordance with the duties imposed on me by honour and royal status with respect to the protection of belief and the promotion of moral good; and with respect to the proclamation of our duties of prayer, almsgiving, fasting, and pilgrimage, and that there is no god but God and that Muhammad is His Prophet, so that no one may be able to blame us for shortcomings in the religion of God; I therefore have deemed it advisable, in addition to giving you the task of constituting your respected corps, to invest you with the right to use advantageous ways and means to investigate these problems carefully and to raise up the light of virtue, and to guide the people to the noble character of their religion and to knowledge of their religious law. You should persevere in this to the utmost and should submit your decisions and recommendations to His most glorious and praiseworthy Eminence our Chief Qadi in order that he also may do what is necessary to carry them out. Keep closely to the Book of God, the conduct (*sunnah*) of the Prophet, and the practices of the imams; they are beacons of knowledge, firm faith, manifest truth, wisdom, guidance, tradition, and understanding.

In this auspicious connection I again remind the honourable cabinet ministers, learned judges, and other civil and military officials of the government that they should represent me truly in my duties toward our religion and in obedience to our Lord. I look upon your deeds with hope and trust, seeking God's help, taking refuge in the illumination of His gracious countenance which has turned darkness to light and which has brought peace both to this world and the next, and asking God to grant success to you and honour and grace to our people. Blessing and peace be upon the guide of his people and Prophet of mercy and upon his pure house and pious companions.

"Labour and God will see your deeds;[6] he who fulfils the task given him by God will receive a great reward."[7]

Issued at Raghadan Palace, Amman

13 Jumada I 1370 (19 February 1951)

[5] Koran 3:100.
[6] Koran 9:106.
[7] Koran 48:10.

Reply of His Eminence
Shaykh Muhammad al-Amin al-Shanqiti

To our Lord, our example, and repository of our hopes:

Your Majesty:

My fellow-ulema and I, servants of the religion of God and the way of your ancestor the Prophet (God's blessing and peace be upon him!), tender Your Majesty our deepest loyalty and most abundant thanks for the precious confidence which you have placed in us and the successive tasks you have delegated to us with respect to a matter that not only concerns this world and its affairs but also one that will be taken into account on the Day of Judgement. You have honoured us, Your Majesty, with abundant grace in assigning us these charges and tasks; may God grant you the best and most gracious of rewards on behalf of ourselves and the people of Islam and tender us success in carrying out the duties you have laid upon us and the programme you have indicated to us.

In accepting this charge, seeking help from God and guidance from Your Majesty, we shall strive, God willing, to make wisdom our guide-post, reason our pathfinder, and divine guidance our leader. Before taking any final decisions we shall submit our findings to our lord and ruler so as to be guided by his keen mind and sound wisdom; he can then order the carrying-out of that which he deems to be urgent and defer that which cannot be carried out for lack of means.

We therefore apply ourselves earnestly to the tasks concerning which you have given commands and suggestions. We trust that God will grant us success in our various undertakings, and we do not doubt that the nation is longing to discharge the obligations which God has laid upon it. We trust also that as a result of Your Majesty's happy intention the nation will follow the ways of its honoured forefathers and turn away from moral standards which are in contradiction to the virtues and teachings of Islam. We do not doubt also that the nation will continue its efforts and endeavour to follow the way of our lord Muhammad (may God bless him and grant him peace!) who said, "I was sent to perfect morals." In this way the nation will gain both this world and the next and will be happy and strong. We ask the Lord (may He be glorified and extolled!) to lengthen the life of Your Majesty, my exalted master, as a treasure, a light, and a refuge for the nation.

Index

Mutayr tribe, 2

Nablus, 21, 32
Nahhas Pasha, Mustafa al-, 7, 8
Najd, 4, 7, 29, 35, 36, 47, 50, 51
  visit to, 50–51
Nashashibi, Raghib Pasha al-, 92, 93
Nasir, Muhammad al-, Lieut. Col., 27
Nazareth, 21
Nazism, 63
Negev, 21
  Egyptian defeat in, 23
Neve Ya'aqov, 74
Night Journey (Mi'raj), 69, 93 and n.
North Africa, 36
Nuqrashi Pasha, al-, 22, 23, 24
Nuri Pasha al-Sa'id, 7

Ottoman Empire, 25, 28, 29, 32, 37, 62
  see also Turkey (Republic)

Pachachi, Muzahim al-, 23 and n., 50 and n.
Pakistan, 51
Palestine, Arab(s), 8, 9, 14, 15, 16ff, 20ff, 30, 33, 34, 35, 37, 46, 50, 68, 73, 74, 77ff
  military operations in, 9ff, 20ff, 33, 50
  problem of, 10ff, 20, 77ff, 89
  see also "Gaza Government",
  immigration, Israel, Jews, Zionism
Palestine Arab Congress, 87 and n.
Paris, 11–12, 28
Passfield, Lord, 80
Peake Pasha, Col., 73
Peel Commission, 85 and n., 88 and n.
Persian Gulf, amirates of, 3
Pilgrimage, the, 5, 65ff, 92
Plumer, Lord, 87
"Portsmouth Treaty", n. 49 ch 1

Qahtan, tribes of, 3
Qawuqji, Fawzi al-, n. 6 ch. 1
Qubbah Palace, al-, 42
Qudsi, Dr Nazim al-, 28ff, 34ff
Quraysh, tribe, 4, 71
Quwwatli, Shukri al-, 20, 27, 33, 50

Raghadan Palace, 96
  minutes of meeting in, 28 and n.
Rahnoma, Zeyn al-'Abidin, 54
Ramallah, 3
Ramlah, al-, 20, 21, 22, 23, 50, 74
Ra's al-'Ayn, 21,
Rashid, House of, 2 and n.
refugees, (refugees question), 12, 15–16, 17, 33
Reza Shah Pahlavi, 56
Rhodes, armistice at, 9, 10, 20
Rifa'i, Samir Pasha al-, 58, 59
Riyad, al-, 23, 68
  visit to, 36 and n.
Russia, 34, 40, 47, 51, 62

Sa'dabad Palace, 56
Safa, al-, 70 and n.
Safad, 21
Saheb-e Garaniyeh Palace, 56
Sa'ib Pasha, General Salih, 23, 24
Sa'id, Dr 'Abd al-Hamid, 77, 86
Sa'id Pasha al-Mufti, 37 and n.
Saladin, 68, 75
Samakh, 21
Samuel, Sir Herbert, 87
San Remo Conference, 53 and n.
Sarah tribes, 2
Sa'ud, Crown Prince, 49
Saudi Arabia, 9
security, collective, 8, 9, 14, 18
Shah of Iran, 54ff, 60
Shahbandar, Dr 'Abd al-Rahman al-, 26
Shahran tribes, 2
Shajarah, al-, 30
Sha'lan Ghalib Bey al-, 73
Shaman, Badri Bey, 52
Shammar tribes, 2
Shanqiti, Shaykh Muhammad al-Amin al-, 95, 97
Sharabati, Ahmad al-, n. 29 ch. 1
Shaykh al-Ard, Nash'at, 26
Shiism, 37, 55
Shishakli, al-, Col., 26, 27
  coup, n. 27 ch. 1
Shurayqi Pasha, Muhammad al-, 53
Silu, Col. Fawzi, 28
Simpson, Sir John Hope, n. 18 ch. 4
Simpson Commission, 88 and n.

101